CHILLI BANANA

AUTHENTIC THAI COOKING
FROM MAY'S KITCHEN

"This book is dedicated to my dear Mother, Jiam Tonggird, from whom I drew my inspiration." - May Wakefield

FOREWORD

FOREWORD, BY JIAM TONGGIRD

Thirty years ago when May and I were cooking together I would never have imagined that the food we made would be written into a book. It is a very overwhelming thing to take in. All of those hours spent in the kitchen teaching and cooking have paid off – including those times when I would tell her off!

I am extremely proud of May. She has learned and accomplished so much in her life, inheriting my own passion and knowledge about food, and taking it from our small corner of Thailand onto bigger and better adventures. May has gone above and beyond my expectations.

Little did I know that Thai food would become so popular around the world. To me, these are simply the recipes we enjoyed cooking, sharing and eating together as a family, and I am delighted that they are now to be shared with so many more people. I wish the best of success for this book, and for May. I hope you enjoy cooking these dishes as much as we have done.

CHILLI BANANA
AUTHENTIC THAI COOKING
FROM MAY'S KITCHEN

ISBN: 978-0-9928981-4-4

Written: May Wakefield, Steven Wakefield,
Rachel Heward
Edited: Phil Turner, Paul Cocker
Proofed: Joe Food, Nick Hallam
Photography: Tim Green
Design: Marc Barker, Paul Cocker
Contributors: Sarah Koriba

Printed by Bell & Bain Ltd, Glasgow

Published by Meze Publishing
Blind Mice Media Ltd
Unit 1 Beehive Works
Milton Street
Sheffield S3 7WL
www.mezepublishing.co.uk
Tel: 0114 275 7709

CONTENTS

MAY'S
JOURNEY

We all have childhood experiences that define us now. Our relationships with our family, friends and loved ones have made us who we are. And I wouldn't be who I am if it wasn't for my mother, who I spent my childhood cooking with back in our village in the Prachinburi farming district, in east Thailand. My mother was a very skilled cook, a talent that was passed down from her mother, who was a widow with eleven children. As my mother was her only daughter, and as is tradition in Thailand, she helped in the kitchen and learned how to cook delicious, traditional and fresh meals for the family every day. My grandmother was cooking even on the very day she passed away, at the age of 97.

My first memory of cooking stems from when I was eleven years old, making curry paste from scratch, blending the ingredients by hand and cutting vegetables to very specific lengths, dictated by my mother. She had certain ways of doing everything, and would always explain why the different vegetables, meat or other ingredients had to be a certain centimetre in length, and why each step, timing and certain techniques were important for that particular dish. My mother's precision, instinct, expertise and passion rivals no one; even now, if we are cooking together she will still be teaching, critiquing and showing me how to do things. Nobody ever stops learning!

From a young age I learned that Thai cooking is all about balance, delicate flavours and most of all, freshness. In our village everything was grown in the back yard, or in the nearby fields and pastures. And whatever fruit, vegetables and herbs you couldn't find nearby, you'd be sure to get at the local market, which also had fresh meat and fish stalls. Just as my grandmother never had a fridge or freezer, we barely even used ours. With everything so close we picked or bought all of our food the same day it was eaten. And with freshness, brings flavour.

I was very lucky to grow up in such a rich area in terms of food produce. Our lifestyle was simple, and we lived to eat. With all of the family living in the same compound, and much of the village's population a stone's throw away, our house was always the hub for social activity, and that activity almost always revolved around the kitchen. The highlight of my childhood and teens was cooking for the family. We'd have banquets, with a huge variety of different kinds of food, from curries to soups, rice, salads and everything in between. Sitting around a big table we would eat slowly, savouring every different flavour, and chat until midnight. For me, food is all about sharing and socialising. This is how I have always known, and always approached cooking.

At each stage of my life I have been cooking for large numbers of people, from helping my mother with family meals and providing food for the farm workers at lunch time, to cooking for friends during my student years, both in Bangkok and in the UK. Whilst studying English literature in Bangkok I met a lot of people from all over the country, and lived with fifteen others. A lot of my friends had little or no cooking experience, so I began teaching them. We would put all of our money into a kitty, and head to the market. A lot of what we bought was food that was likely to be thrown out the next day, so we honed our bartering skills and began collecting fruit and vegetables for very little money. This meant we were able to buy fresh meat, fish and herbs; it was a cooking challenge to create tasty dishes on a budget, from whatever we could get our hands on from the market. At the weekend I would go home and cook with my mother. We'd plan banquets and nobody in our family would ever miss them if they could help it; even if my father was to dine out as part of a work meeting, he would only eat a small amount, and have his main meal at home.

I went to London to study and it is here that my cooking ventures took me even further. Thai food was relatively unknown at the time, and my cooking soon became popular as people were impressed by the fresh and flavoursome variety of food. I would be invited to cook at parties, for friends and even teachers. Trying food from other cultures opens people's minds, becomes a talking point and offers an insight into a different way of life. As it was

at home, my social life revolved around cooking, eating and sharing.

When I'd completed my studies, I went back to Thailand, much to my family's delight, although I had in my mind a plan to go back to the UK and study something related to my passion for cooking. My mother always wanted me to use my English, and my degree. She didn't see cooking as a future career. Yet my father, who was more liberal, persuaded her to let me go once more to the UK, this time to Manchester, to study a hospitality and catering course. It was here that I learned from other cultures and added flavours and ingredients I had never come across before. Every Friday we

had a night where a lot of the foreign students got together to cook and share food. Trying cuisine from other countries influenced my imagination hugely, and I experimented with flavours and ingredients not usually found in Thailand.

It was also in Manchester that I met my husband-to-be, Steve, who was working in a Thai restaurant and shared an equal passion for food. On a trip to Kent one day, we came across a restaurant with a sign outside saying 'Thai Food Served Here' and, although closed, we popped around the back and had a chat and ended up having some delicious, but simple food. This was our 'Eureka' moment. We could do

this, and maybe better... Two weeks later we had found the place and we were open. It was a Thursday. I was born on a Thursday, and my mother has always said if you start something on this day, all will be well.

That was in 1996, and until November 2013, Chilli Banana was happily situated in Alderley Edge, in a small restaurant attached to a pub. Our new premises spans two floors and boasts a state of the art open kitchen. Three thousand handmade bricks were shipped from Ayutthaya in the Chao Phraya Valley and Thai furnishings, art and decorations came 6,000 miles by container ship, creating an authentic Asian atmosphere.

The name emphasises the importance of the food itself, and unlike many other east Asian restaurants, which are often named 'Royal' or 'Palace' something, we wanted a way of creatively showing what we were all about. There's nothing 'royal' about the food, everything is authentic, Thai cooking, focusing on freshness and flavour above anything else. While we create dishes that you may find in the skyscraper restaurants towering above Bangkok, there are also plenty of humble, yet delicious street food dishes. The standard of street food in Thailand is excellent, and what you lack in presentation you get back in flavour. Chilli Banana suggests a crossover of flavours, of sweet and spicy and a blend and balance of two opposites. This is exactly what we do; we have a variety of dishes, from the complex to the simple, from sweet to spicy and everything in between. And yes, we do have a signature dish using both chillies and bananas.

Now, on top of Chilli Banana in Wilmslow, we also have two franchises in the North West, in Liverpool and Macclesfield. We go back to Thailand several times a year in order to stay in touch with food trends, and to keep the style, culture and heart of home in everything that you can taste in our restaurants.

This book is a dedication to my mother, Jiam. Her recipes have never been written down and this is my way of preserving the memories of our cooking together, all of those years ago. I know how proud my mother is of what I have achieved and accomplished, and it has all been because of her. If she never taught me how to make my first curry paste, we wouldn't be here now.

Throughout this book you'll find tips, facts and guidelines to accompany the recipes which are organised in sections from appetisers and light bites to stir-fries, curries, seafood, rice & noodles and desserts. For any Thai ingredients that are not part of your usual supermarket shop, take a look at the 'Trip To The Market' chapter, which will point you in the right direction.

Use your senses. With Thai cooking it's all about trusting your instincts; the aroma the food produces, the sound it makes and the colours and textures will tell and show you exactly how the food is supposed to be. Above all, taste, taste and taste again. You can adjust most of the recipes according to your preferences, so you can't really go wrong.

As we shared our food back home around that long table, we are sharing our food now with hundreds of others. We hope you enjoy this book as much as we've enjoyed creating the recipes together.

A TRIP TO THE MARKET

I love the hustle and bustle of a trip to the market to get ingredients for the day's cooking. Gossip and friendly banter are ever present as you jostle for position with barrow boys and other shoppers whilst working your way up and down the narrow walkways, between stalls piled high with the wonderful and exotic produce that Thailand has to offer.

Whilst lacking the atmosphere of my local market, there are very good Thai, Oriental or Chinese supermarkets in which the following ingredients are available. A good proportion of these can even be found in your local supermarket. You can always order from one of the many specialist online Thai stores for convenience or if you can't find them locally.

Ka – Galangal

Similar to ginger in appearance, but with a pinkish colour and a more subtle flavour. Galangal is one of the main ingredients in Tom Yam and Tom Ka soups, when paired with lemongrass. Available fresh.

Takrai – Lemongrass

These fibrous stalks have a wonderful citrus flavour when broken or sliced.

King – Ginger

A popular root herb used in stir-fries and some seafood dishes. As it gets older it becomes more fibrous and has a stronger taste.

Prik Thai Sot – Fresh green peppercorns

These grow on a creeper plant with the peppercorns dangling in rows. They have a fiery pepper flavour and are one of the main ingredients of 'Jungle curry'.

Bai Makrut – Kaffir lime leaves

The leaves of the kaffir lime tree are used extensively in Thai cooking. Giving a fuller citrus flavour they are used in soups, stir-fries, curry pastes as well as the fried, crispy version garnishing many dishes. Available frozen.

Horapa – Thai sweet basil leaves

This has an intense aniseed flavour. It is used mainly in curries and stir-fries and should be added at the end as it should not be cooked for too long.

Peuw Makrut – Kaffir lime skin

Kaffir limes have an unusually knobbly skin. Used in making curry paste, as the skin provides a full citrus flavour. Sometimes available frozen.

Keun Chai – Thai celery

Smaller in size yet stronger in taste than celery available in the UK. It is an important ingredient in some Thai salads.

Gui Chai – Thai chives

A long thin leaf with a garlic flavour, it is the green leaf used in the famous Pad Thai noodles. It is often substituted with spring onions.

Bai Salanair – Mint

Fresh mint is readily available in grocers and supermarkets.

akua Puang – Pea aubergines

hey look like large peas but are a more like a miniature
ggplant with seeds inside. They are cooked in curry dishes
nd are quite hard with a bitter taste.

Krachai

This is a root herb in the
ginger family, but with
a much stronger, more
distinctive flavour. It is the
star of 'Jungle Curry'.

Cumin Sot - Fresh turmeric

Another member of the
ginger family. It is very
common in southern Thai
dishes.

Raag Pak Chee – Coriander roots

The roots of the coriander
plant are used for flavouring
soups, stocks and curry
pastes.

Pak Chee Farang – Thai parsley (sawtooth coriander)

A leaf herb with a distinctive
serrated edge, hence the
name. It is in the coriander
family and has a stronger
taste than normal coriander.

akua Plo – Thai eggplant

an be eaten raw or cooked in curries. They have a slightly
tter taste.

Krapow – Thai holy basil leaves

These leaves have a clove-
like peppery fragrance,
and unlike sweet basil,
they need to be cooked to
release its flavour.

Prik Haeng – Dried chilli

The chilli equivalent of a sun dried tomato. Sun drying the chilli gives it a wonderful flavour. Large ones are used in stir-fries or for the base of the curry paste. Small ones are ground up to make dried chilli powder – a jar of which can be found on the table of every restaurant or café in Thailand.

Prik Chee Faa Daeng – Long red chilli

Not as hot as the bird's eye chilli. Can be de-seeded to reduce the heat further. Used as decoration, in stir-fries, or to make sauces.

Prik Bun – Dried chilli powder

Ground sun dried chilli. This powdered chilli is served alongside seasoning in restaurants and cafés in Thailand to spice up food to your required level.

Prik Kii Noo Sot – Thai chilli

Chillies are used extensively in Thai cooking. They start life green and turn red when ripe. These are 2-3cm long and very hot.

Si Racha sauce

This is a great tasting chilli sauce which can be used for seafood and meats alike. It originates from the town of the same name. There are different strengths available.

Palm Sugar

Rich creamy sugar produced from the sap of the sugar palm tree. Comes in handy sized 'cakes'.

Si Yew Kao - Light soy sauce

This is widely used for seasoning. It is salty, light coloured and has a distinctive flavour. It is also served as a condiment to add a salty flavour to food after cooking.

Si Yew Dam - Dark soy sauce

This is richer, slightly sweeter and less salty in flavour than light soy. Its flavour is developed when heated and it adds colour to the food.

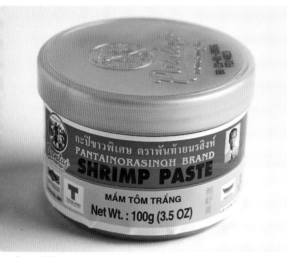

Curry paste

It's always nicer to make fresh, but if you don't have time some very good ones are available from supermarkets and oriental stores.

...api – Shrimp paste

...his pungent smelling shrimp-based product is used in ...mall amounts to add flavour to pastes and dishes.

Makharm – Tamarind

The pulp of the tamarind plant is available in sticky blocks. They normally contain the seeds which will need to be strained out during cooking.

Nam Pla - Fish sauce

The main source of salty flavour in Thai food. Made from fermented anchovies, it has an intense salty taste. Most brands are similar in flavour.

Normai - Bamboo shoots

At home in Thailand bamboo shoots are harvested early in the mornings and eaten fresh during the day. Only available in tins. Look for them cut into strips.

...ati - Coconut milk

...oconut milk is a liquid ...repared from the white ...esh in coconuts. Best ...ought in the tinned variety. ...trengths and tastes vary ...etween brands.

Kratiem Dong - Pickled garlic

Pickled garlic is not as strong in taste as fresh garlic, but has a wonderful tangy taste. Available in jars from your local Oriental supermarket.

Naman Hoy - Oyster sauce

Used for stir-fires and marinating. Always use a good quality oyster sauce.

STARTERS & LIGHT BITES

You can't walk far down the pavement in Thailand without the aroma of food from a cooking cart spiking the air. Thailand is, after all, the home of snacking and street food. In this land where food punctuates daily life, tasty bites are always on hand to satisfy your hunger – at any time of the day or night.

These street-side morsels have now developed into entrees in the modern day Thai restaurant, but are still terrific snacks in their own right.

เสือร้องไห้
SUA RONG HAI
TIGER'S TEARS

Traditionally in Thailand, the beef was barbecued over charcoal and the drips of fat into the fire were likened to tiger's tears.

INGREDIENTS

250g sirloin steak, 2.5 cm thick

½ tbsp soy sauce

A few drops of vegetable oil, for rubbing

1 tbsp Nam Jim Jaew dipping sauce (see page 185)

METHOD

Using the grill on maximum, heat a griddle pan or heavy frying pan for a few minutes until really hot.

Meanwhile, rub the light soy sauce and oil into the steak.

Put the steak in the pan and place under the heat.

For medium-rare, cook for 2 minutes on each side

For medium, cook for 2½ minutes on each side.

Slice the steak across in slices around 5-10 mm.

Serve with the Nam Jim Jaew dipping sauce.

CHEF'S TIP

When eating, dip into the sauce rather than pouring it over the meat.

PREPARATION TIME:	COOKING TIME	SERVES	SPICE RATING
10 MINS	4-5 MINS	2 PEOPLE	

สะเต๊ะไก่
SATAY GAI
CHICKEN SATAY

This is a very popular dish, and is often eaten as a snack, although it is great as a starter to share.

INGREDIENTS

500g chicken breast

½ tbsp cumin powder

1 tbsp turmeric powder

40g coriander seeds, finely ground

1 tsp salt

80g sugar

160ml coconut milk

80ml evaporated carnation milk

60ml vegetable oil

TO SERVE

Nam Jim Satay, peanut sauce (see page 187)

Nam Jim Arjard, cucumber and red onion relish (see page 186)

METHOD

Cut the chicken into ½cm slices about 5-7cm in width.

Put all of the ingredients, except the chicken, in a mixing bowl.

Mix well, making sure the sugar has dissolved.

Break up all the lumps from the herb powder.

Add the chicken and leave to marinate for about 2-3 hours, or preferably overnight.

Preheat the grill to maximum.

Meanwhile, skewer the chicken on bamboo skewers.

Lay them neatly on a rack on an oven tray. When the grill is hot, put the chicken tray on the top shelf.

Grill for 4-5 minutes.

Take it out to turn them over to the other side. Do not leave the oven door open as the temperature has to remain hot.

Cook for a few more minutes.

Using a sharp knife to cut through a piece, check whether the chicken pieces are done.

When they are white in the middle, they will be cooked through. If pink, cook a bit longer.

Serve with peanut sauce and cucumber and red onion relish.

| PREPARATION TIME: 30 MINS PLUS 2-3 HOURS OR OVERNIGHT | COOKING TIME 6-7 MINS | SERVES 8-10 PEOPLE | SPICE RATING |

หมูปิ้ง
MOO PING

PORK ON SKEWERS GRILLES OR BARBECUED

These succulent skewers are a great starter or can be eaten with sticky rice and dipping sauce as an easy meal.

INGREDIENTS

500g pork loin or chump steak

10g garlic

10g fresh coriander roots or storks, finely cut

A few black peppercorns, finely ground

40g sugar

2 tbsp oyster sauce

2 tbsp light soy sauce

2 tsp dark soy sauce

2-3 tbsp vegetable oil

2 tbsp evaporated carnation milk

3 tbsp thickest part of coconut milk

TO SERVE

Nam Jim Buay, sweet chilli plum dipping sauce (see page 187)

METHOD
TO MARINATE

Cut the pork into thin slices about 5-7cm in width.

Wash and leave to drain really well then place them in a big mixing bowl.

Put the garlic and coriander into a heavy mortar and pound them until quite fine.

Add the ground black pepper and sugar in, then pound again.

Add all of the ingredients in with the pork and mix them together by hand (preferably using disposable gloves).

Make sure all of the herbs are not in a big clump and that the sugar is dissolved.

Cover and leave to marinate for at least 2 hours, or preferably overnight.

Once marinated, skewer the pork pieces.

Preheat the grill to maximum.

Put all the skewers on a grill rack evenly and cook for 3 minutes, turn, then cook for a further 3 minutes, or until cooked.

Check the thickest pieces, leave any uncooked ones to cook and remove the pieces that are ready.

Alternatively, barbecue over charcoal.

| PREPARATION TIME: 2 HOURS OR MARINATE OVERNIGHT | COOKING TIME 6-7 MINS | SERVES 6 PEOPLE | SPICE RATING |

ปอเปี๊ยทอด
PO PIA TOD
THAI SPRING ROLLS

Perfect as a starter or a snack with sweet chilli dipping sauce. The spring roll pastries can easily be defrosted at room temperature whilst preparing the filling.

INGREDIENTS

85g minced chicken

100g hard white cabbage, cut into thin long strips

25g carrots, peeled and shredded into long strips

1 tbsp vegetable oil

1 tsp garlic, finely chopped

1 tbsp light soy sauce

¼ tsp ground white pepper

¼ tsp sugar

60g vermicelli noodles

1 pack frozen spring roll pastry, 10-12cm square

1 tbsp plain flour

1 tbsp water

2-3 cups vegetable oil

TO SERVE

Nam Jim Wan, sweet chilli sauce (see page 187)

METHOD

Soak the vermicelli noodles with lukewarm water until soft. This takes about 30 minutes with cold water.

Drain all of the water off and cut into 12-15cm lengths.

Thaw the frozen pastry naturally, in a fridge overnight or for 30 minutes at room temperature.

In a wok on a high heat, stir the minced chicken in oil and add the chopped garlic.

Use a spatula to break up the chicken quickly. Do not let it form into big pieces.

Once the chicken is cooked, season with the light soy sauce, sugar and pepper, stirring all the time.

Add the cabbage and carrot. Stir and mix well until the vegetables are cooked, al dente. Do not overcook the vegetables as some juice will be released, making it too moist.

Put the well-drained vermicelli in and mix well until the noodles are cooked and soft. This process doesn't take long.

Make sure the mixture is dry to help prevent the pastry splitting.

You should now have about 350g of cooked mixture.

Put the mixture onto a large flat plate to cool.

Peel the pastry out one by one and wrap them with a damp tea towel.

Mix the plain flour and water until dissolved to make a paste.

Use about 13-15g or one tablespoon for each sheet of defrosted pastry. Place the mixture a third of the way up in the pastry.

Fold the pastry upward to cover the mixture then fold two sides in. Then roll to make a spring roll, using a little of the plain flour mixture to stick down the top corner of pastry (see picture).

This mixture will make approximately 25-30 mini spring rolls.

Heat the cooking oil on medium to high heat, making sure it does not go smoky.

Prepare a tray or bowl lined with a few pieces of kitchen paper.

Heat the oil in a wok, put a few spring rolls in and fry until golden brown. Remove from the heat into the prepared tray or bowl

Serve with sweet chilli sauce.

PREPARATION TIME:	COOKING TIME	SERVES	SPICE RATING
45 MINS	10 MINS	4 PEOPLE	🌶🌶🌶

เนื้อแดดเดียว
NUA DET DEOW
MARINATED STEAK STRIPS

INGREDIENTS

250g lean rump steak, cut into
5-7cm length strips at 1cm thick

½ tbsp light soy sauce

1 tbsp oyster sauce

1 tsp sesame oil

1 tsp sugar

3 tbsp vegetable oil

TO GARNISH

¼ tsp roasted sesame seeds

TO SERVE

Nam Jim Talay, chilli & garlic
dipping sauce (see page 186)

Sriracha sauce

Traditionally the meat is left to marinate in the sun
for one day, hence the name Nua Det Deow which
translates as 'one sun dried beef'.

METHOD

Put all the ingredients together in a bowl and mix well.

Marinate it for at least 1 hour or put cling film over the bowl
and keep in the fridge overnight.

Once marinated, heat the oil in a wok on medium heat.

When the oil is quite hot but not smoky, put all of the steak
in.

Stir continuously, making sure all of the steak strips are
evenly cooked. This should take about 3 minutes.

Take them off the hot oil. Put in them in a bowl lined with
kitchen paper to drain the oil off.

Serve on a warm plate and sprinkle the roasted sesame
seeds over. Serve with spicy garlic dipping sauce.

PREPARATION TIME:	COOKING TIME	SERVES	SPICE RATING
10 MINS PLUS 1 HOUR FOR MARINATING	3-5 MINS	2-3 PEOPLE	🌶🌶🌶

ไก่ห่อใบเตย
GAI HAW BI-TEUY
CHICKEN WRAPPED IN PANDAN LEAVES

INGREDIENTS

500g chicken, cut into 2.5cm cubed pieces

1 small clove garlic

2-3 black peppercorns

5g coriander roots or stalks

¼ tsp sugar

1 tbsp sesame oil

1 tbsp oyster sauce

1 tbsp tomato ketchup

1 tbsp light soy sauce

¼ tsp cumin powder

⅔ tbsp white onion, very finely chopped

2 cups vegetable oil, for deep frying

16 pandan leaves, cut diagonally into 30cm long pieces

FOR THE SAUCE

2 tbsp Nam Makharm, tamarind syrup sauce (see page 186)

1/8 tsp roasted dry chilli flake

¼ tsp roasted sesame seed

The pandan leaves are not to be eaten, but will add a delicious nutty kind of flavour, complementing the marinated chicken perfectly.

METHOD

In a granite mortar, pound the garlic, black peppercorns and coriander together until very fine.

Add into the mixing bowl with the rest of the ingredients.

Mix them very well by hand. Make sure all of the powder and herbs coat the chicken evenly.

Leave the mixture to marinate for at least 2 hours, but preferably overnight.

Wrap a cube of chicken into 2 pieces of pandan leaves (see picture).

Tighten each one well and place them in a heatproof bowl, ready for steaming.

Put at least 20cm of water in the bottom of a steamer, cover and bring to boil over a high heat.

Place the bowl on the rack in the steamer and cover with a lid. Steam for about 8-10 minutes.

Turn the heat off and put the steamed chicken wraps onto a tray laid with kitchen paper.

Pat dry any excess juice from the steamed chicken wraps.

Heat the oil on a medium to high heat.

When the oil is hot, put the steamed chicken in, a few at a time.

Use a long frying tool if possible, as there might be a splash of hot oil from the wok.

It will take a few minutes to get the pandan leaves crispy and the outer parts of the chicken slightly brown.

Using a slatted spoon, remove the fried chicken from the hot oil and lay on a prepared tray with kitchen paper to drain off any oil.

Mix all of the sauce ingredients together and serve with the chicken.

PREPARATION TIME: 20 MINS (PLUS TIME TO MARINATE OVERNIGHT)	COOKING TIME 15 MINS	SERVES 3-4 PEOPLE	SPICE RATING 🌶🌶🌶

ทอดมันปลา
TOD MAN PLA
SPICY FISHCAKES

These spicy fishcakes are delicious with a cooling cucumber relish. By mixing the French beans and kaffir lime leaves in at the end, you'll get a lovely crunchy texture as well.

INGREDIENTS

250g cod fillet, cut into small chunks

250g hake fillet, cut into small chunks

40-50g red curry paste

10g kaffir lime leaves, stork removed and torn into small pieces

2 tsp sugar

2 tsp paprika powder

1 large egg

½ tsp fish sauce

50g French beans, finely cut crossways

5g kaffir lime leaves, very thinly sliced

1 litre vegetable oil, for frying

TO SERVE

2 tbsp Nam Jim Arjard, pickled cucumber (see page 186)

1 tbsp Nam Jim Buay (see page 187)

½ tsp ground peanuts

CHEF'S TIPS

Once the fishcake mixture is fine, do not continue blending, as this will create moisture in the mixture and the fried fishcake will be wet inside with a rubbery outer skin.

Make sure you have the right utensils (such as a slotted spoon) to deep fry and a tray lined with kitchen paper to absorb any excess oil.

METHOD

Put all of the ingredients except the fish sauce, French beans and thinly sliced kaffir lime leaves, into a large food processor.

Blend it until fine and well mixed.

Check that there are no large pieces of fish undone and that all herbs and spices are well blended in.

Do not worry if the spices are not blended in evenly through the fishcake mixture.

Remove from the food processor and transfer the mixture into a large bowl.

Wear a pair of disposable gloves and mix by hand like you are kneading dough.

Add the prepared French beans and kaffir lime leaves, but not the fish sauce at this point as some batches of curry paste can be saltier than others.

Knead again to mix everything together.

Taste by frying a small piece of mixture in hot oil, being careful not to let it get smoky.

Now add the required amount of fish sauce and mix really well again.

Form the mixture into about 20-25g balls then place on a well-oiled tray. Do not let them stick together.

Preheat the oil in a wok on high heat. Do not let it get smoky as this will burn the outer fishcake and French beans, but leave the inside uncooked.

Meanwhile, flatten the fish balls into less than 1cm thick fishcakes.

Cover with a sheet of cling film if not ready to fry yet.

When ready, add the fishcakes to the oil one by one.

Once a fishcake begins to float, turn. This will happen after only 1-2 minutes.

Slowly add more pieces and repeat until finished.

Try to maintain the oil temperature by not putting too many pieces in at once.

It only takes a maximum of 3 minutes to achieve an even colour in each piece.

If it gets too hot and smoky, turn the heat down, wait until the smoke disappears and it returns to the right temperature.

To make the cucumber relish, mix the cucumber pickle and sweet chilli sauce together then sprinkle with the ground peanut.

Serve hot and accompany with cucumber relish.

PREPARATION TIME:	COOKING TIME	SERVES	SPICE RATING
30 MINS, PLUS 25 MINUTES FOR CURRY PASTE	3-4 MINS	10-12 PEOPLE	🌶🌶🌶

HOY NANG ROM NEUNG

STEAMED OYSTERS WITH CHILLI GARLIC SAUCE AND CRISPY FRIED SHALLOTS

INGREDIENTS

6 fresh Scottish or Cornish oysters

6 tsp Nam Jim Talay, chilli garlic dipping sauce (see page 186)

6 tsp Hom Jeow, crispy fried shallots (see page 187)

An incredible taste sensation, and a personal favourite. The steamed, fresh oysters are perfect with the chilli garlic sauce and then you get a wonderful aftertaste of fried shallots.

METHOD

Clean the oysters by scrubbing them under a cold tap.

With a sharp and narrow knife find the opening between the two shells and work the blade in. Once inside, slide the blade along the inside of the top shell to allow it to open. Remove the top shell and slide the knife under the oyster to release it from the lower shell. Leave in the shell.

Add 5cm of water to the steamer and bring to rapid boil on a high heat.

Arrange the oysters, in the lower shells, in the steamer trivet. Put in the steamer, cover, and steam for 2-3 minutes. Be careful not to overcook and shrink the oysters, they should still be nice and soft.

When cooked, remove from the steamer and drain off any water, leaving the oysters in the shells.

Spoon one teaspoon of chilli garlic dipping sauce, and one teaspoon of crispy fried shallots, over each oyster and serve.

PREPARATION TIME:	COOKING TIME	SERVES	SPICE RATING
10 MINS	2-3 MINS	2 PEOPLE	🌶🌶🌶

ทอดมันกุ้ง
TOD MAN GUNG
PRAWN CAKES

A lovely alternative to crab or white fishcakes. Perfect for sharing and dipping into sweet chilli sauce.

INGREDIENTS

500g prawns, shelled and de-veined

½ tsp salt

½ tsp ground white pepper

½ egg white

¾ tbsp sesame oil

¾ tbsp potato starch

FOR COATING

1 cup of fresh or dry breadcrumbs

3-4 cups vegetable oil, for frying

TO SERVE

Nam Jim Buay, sweet chilli sauce with preserved plum (see page 187)

CHEF'S TIP

You can prepare the prawn mixture in advance, form them into balls and keep in the fridge for up to 24 hours.

Do not coat with breadcrumbs until you are ready to deep fry them and serve immediately.

METHOD

Mix all of the ingredients really well in a mixing bowl, by hand at first.

Then mix them again in a food processor and blend for about 1-2 minutes.

Make sure the mixture does not go too fine.

Remove the prawn mixture into the previous mixing bowl.

Form the prawn mixture into equal shapes, about the size of a golf ball, around 20-25g per each one.

Place them on a flat tray.

Thinly spread half of the breadcrumbs across another tray.

Flatten each prawn ball down to about 1cm thick and 5cm wide.

Lay each one on top of prepared breadcrumbs. Do not put them on top of each other as they will stick together.

Now sprinkle the rest of breadcrumbs on the top of the uncooked prawn cakes.

Heat a deep wok on a medium heat and put the oil in.

Wait until the oil is quite hot but not smoky.

If it is too hot the breadcrumbs will burn before the prawn cakes are cooked all the way through.

Make sure the oil is also deep enough for the prawn cake to be submerged by using a spatula to hold it down.

It should take about 2-3 minutes on each side or until just golden brown. Be careful not to overcook, as the cake will expand and will be tough on the outside.

Serve immediately with sweet chilli sauce.

PREPARATION TIME:	COOKING TIME	SERVES	SPICE RATING
30 MINS	4-5 MINS	8 PEOPLE	🌶🌶🌶

GUNG POW

GRILLED KING PRAWNS ON SKEWERS

Whilst relaxing on any of Thailand's popular beaches, it won't be too long before you are approached by a vendor, with a mobile barbecue, offering simple seafood cooked right in front of you. The combination of fresh seafood and spicy dipping sauce is unbeatable.

INGREDIENTS

5-10 king prawns, de-veined and with the tail left on

1 tsp light soy sauce

1-2 tsp vegetable oil

TO SERVE

Nam Jim Talay, spicy fresh garlic dipping sauce (see page 186)

METHOD

Preheat the grill to maximum heat.

Meanwhile, skewer the prepared king prawns onto each skewer, putting the tail on first.

Rub in the soy sauce and vegetable oil.

Arrange them on a rack on top of an oven tray.

When the grill is hot, put the tray on the top shelf.

Grill for 4-5 minutes, depending on the size of the prawn.

Take it out to check quickly, but do not leave the grill door open as it might need longer to cook. The temperature has to remain hot.

If the prawns turn orange, they are cooked.

If they are still white in colour, or transparent and soft, then put back under the grill for 1-2 minutes until cooked.

Do not cook them for too long as they will go dry and hard.

Grilled prawns should be orange, not a dry brown in colour, and they should be succulent inside.

Serve immediately while still hot with nam jim talay, a spicy fresh garlic dipping sauce.

PREPARATION TIME:	COOKING TIME	SERVES	SPICE RATING
5-10 MINS	5-6 MINS	1-2 PEOPLE	🌶🌶🌶

58

ตับไก่ย่าง
DAB GAI YANG
GRILLED MARINATED CHICKEN LIVERS

INGREDIENTS

150g chicken livers, washed and drained

15g coriander roots

2 small cloves garlic

2 black peppercorns

1 tsp sugar

2 tbsp oyster sauce

½ tbsp vegetable oil

TO SERVE

Nam Jim Buay, sweet chilli and pickled plum sauce (see page 187)

If you like chicken livers, you will love these delicious marinated livers grilled on skewers.

METHOD

Pound coriander, garlic and black pepper together in a mortar and pestle until quite fine.

Put all of the ingredients in a mixing bowl and mix well by hand, but gently. Cover the bowl with cling film and leave to marinate in a fridge for half an hour.

Preheat the grill to maximum until very hot.

Put all of the marinated chicken livers on a fine rack, or skewer the pieces of chicken liver on bamboo skewers – this will make the meat easier to turn during cooking.

Lay the skewers on a rack and spread them neatly so they will be evenly cooked.

Place the rack on the top of a heatproof tray.

Once the grill is extremely hot, insert the tray onto the grill shelf.

Grill for 4 minutes at first and quickly turn them over and put back to cook for a further 3-4 minutes. The outside will have a nice char but the inside will be left pink. Grill longer if you prefer your meat well done.

Transfer the livers on to a warm plate and serve with Nam Jim Buay sweet chilli and pickled plum sauce.

PREPARATION TIME:	COOKING TIME	SERVES	SPICE RATING
45 MINS	9-10 MINS	1-2 PEOPLE	🌶🌶🌶

SOUPS

Soups are very popular in Thailand, whether it be one of the many varieties of noodle soup eaten by millions on their lunch break, a hearty rice soup for breakfast or a richer tom yam or tom ka with their flavours of infused herbs.

ต้มยำกุ้งน้ำข้น
TOM YAM GUNG NAM KON
HOT AND SOUR PRAWN SOUP
WITH OYSTER MUSHROOMS

INGREDIENTS

6-8 king prawns, shelled, de-veined, tail left on

2 cups water

1 stork lemongrass, cut into 2.5cm length

6-8 thinly sliced galangal pieces

2 Kaffir lime leaves, torn into small pieces

1 fresh Thai red chilli, coarsely crushed

1½ tbsp fish sauce

25g oyster mushrooms, torn into 2.5cm wide pieces

¾ tbsp fresh lime juice

2 tbsp evaporated carnation milk

¼ tsp Nam Prik Pow, chilli oil (see page 186)

TO GARNISH

Sprig of coriander

CHEF'S TIP

Freshly squeezed lime juice will make all the difference to the Tom Yam. If you like it hot, then just add more fresh chilli, but in doing so you should also increase the fish sauce and the lime juice in order to keep a well balanced flavour.

This soup is a thicker version of the traditional Tom Yam style. If you prefer a clear stock, just leave the carnation milk and chilli oil out.

METHOD

In a saucepan bring the water to boil on a high heat. Add the lemongrass, galangal, kaffir lime leaves, chilli and fish sauce.

Allow the herbs to infuse for 30 seconds.

Drop the prawns in slowly, making sure the stock is continually boiling.

After 2-3 minutes, the prawns should have turned pink.

Then add the mushrooms and take off the heat.

In a serving bowl, add the fresh lime juice, chilli oil and carnation milk. Pour in the soup and garnish with fresh coriander.

PREPARATION TIME:	COOKING TIME	SERVES	SPICE RATING
10 MINS	5 MINS	2 PEOPLE	🌶🌶🌶

ก๋วยเตี๋ยวน้ำหมู
GOYTEOW NAM MOO
NOODLE SOUP WITH PORK

Fresh and healthy fast food – Thai style. Millions of bowls of noodle soup are eaten every day in Thailand. There are many different choices of noodle along with meat, duck, chicken or seafood with each shop having their own special 'house' combination. Here we have a classic pork noodle soup with 'Sen Lek' – thin rice noodles.

INGREDIENTS

FOR THE STOCK

1 large clove garlic, peeled

10g coriander root

3 slices mooli, 1cm thick, peeled

1 tsp salt

2 tsp sugar

3 tbsp light soy sauce

3 tbsp oyster sauce

250g spare ribs chopped into 4cm

FOR THE SOUP

200g rice sticks, 3mm (soaked overnight in cold water and drained. If you are short of time, soak in hot water until soft and then rinse well)

75g fresh beansprouts

150g pork loin, thinly sliced

3 tsp Kratiem Grob, crispy fried garlic (see page 186)

30g chopped spring onion

30g chopped Thai celery

CONDIMENTS

2 tbsp white vinegar

½ long red chilli thinly sliced

2 tsp sugar

METHOD

TO MAKE THE STOCK

In a large saucepan, add all of the ingredients apart from the spare ribs to 1 litre of water and bring to the boil.

Then add the spare ribs and simmer for 30 minutes. Taste and season if required.

To prepare the condiments, combine the vinegar and sliced long red chilli in a small bowl. Place the sugar, fish sauce and chilli flakes into individual small bowls.

TO MAKE THE SOUP

While the stock is simmering prepare all of the soup ingredients.

Just before the stock is ready, bring 500ml water to the boil in a second saucepan.

Using a small sieve, poach the beansprouts for 30 seconds, remove, drain and divide them between 3 pre-warmed soup bowls.

Using the same hot water, poach the rice sticks for 1-2 minutes until soft, but not mushy. Drain well in a colander and quickly divide and place on top of the beansprouts in the bowls.

Using the sieve, poach the pork in the simmering stock and again divide between the 3 bowls, placing on top of the noodles.

Ladle enough stock over the contents of the bowl so they are just covered.

Finally divide the crispy garlic, chopped spring onion and Thai celery into 3 and sprinkle over to garnish.

Serve immediately.

Taste and season to your individual taste by using the condiments.

PREPARATION TIME:	COOKING TIME	SERVES	SPICE RATING
OVERNIGHT FOR SOAKING	40 MINS	3 PEOPLE	🌶🌶🌶

ไก่ต้มข่า

GAI TOM KA

CHICKEN AND CAULIFLOWERS IN COCONUT MILK SOUP

INGREDIENTS

80g chicken breast, thinly sliced

80g cauliflower, cut into small florets

½-¾ tin coconut milk

10g lemongrass, cut into 2.5cm pieces

10g galangal, thinly sliced

2 kaffir lime leaves, torn into small pieces

½ fresh Thai chilli, coarsely crushed

1 tbsp fish sauce

1 tsp fresh lime juice

TO GARNISH

A sprig of fresh coriander

CHEF'S TIP

Always use freshly squeezed lime juice, as this will really set off the flavours of the soup.

This fragrant soup is versatile; ideal as a quick dinner or light lunch for one, yet easily altered for more.

METHOD

Put coconut milk in a saucepan on a high heat.

Add lemongrass, galangal, kaffir lime leaves, fish sauce and chilli. Allow to infuse for 1 minute and for the soup to boil.

Add chicken and cauliflowers at same time. Bring it to boil then immediately reduce the heat and simmer for further 2-3 minutes, until the chicken is cooked and the cauliflower is al-dente.

Add the freshly squeezed lime juice to a warm serving bowl and pour in the soup.

Garnish with coriander and serve.

PREPARATION TIME:	COOKING TIME	SERVES	SPICE RATING
10 MINS	4-5 MINS	1 PERSON	

TOM MA-RA KRADOOK ON

BITTER MELON SOUP WITH SPARE RIBS

INGREDIENTS

350-400g bitter melon

500g spare ribs, chopped into 4cm pieces

2 large garlic cloves

10 black peppercorns

25g shallots

10g coriander root

4 tbsp light soy sauce

3 pints water

Bitter melon is an acquired taste but has become a firm favourite of mine! It is an unusual soup, with a hint of bitterness at first but with a lovely natural sweet stock flavour in it as well.

METHOD

Put the water into a medium saucepan on a high heat.

Season with soy sauce. In a mortar, pound the black peppercorn roughly.

Add the coriander, garlic and shallots and gently pound in together. This is just to break the herbs up.

Add the herbs in the stock saucepan and bring the soup stock to boil.

While the herbs are left to infuse their flavour, wash and drain the spare ribs well. Then add the ribs, one by one, into the boiling stock. This will prevent the stock from turning cloudy and keep it to the boiling point.

Skim any foam off the stock surface to keep the stock nice and clear. Repeat from time to time if necessary.

Put a lid on, but leave a little gap for the steam to breathe.

Leave it simmering on a medium heat for about 45 minutes, and be careful not to over boil.

Meanwhile, wash and cut the bitter melon into about 5cm pieces. Scrape out the seeds and soft centre parts. Wash and drain well.

Take a piece of spare rib meat and use a knife to cut through to check its tenderness.

When the spare ribs are soft and tender, bring the stock to rapid boil.

Gently put all of the prepared bitter melon in and bring to boil again. Do not put a lid on.

Leave it on medium heat until the bitter melon is soft and cooked through.

This process may take up to 15-20 minutes.

The soup will become slightly cloudy but be careful not to overcook the bitter melon.

Taste. It should only be slightly bitter at first, but with a natural sweet stock flavour layered in.

Serve hot.

PREPARATION TIME:	COOKING TIME	SERVES	SPICE RATING
20 MINS	1 HOUR	3-4 PEOPLE	)))

ต้มยำปลาบึก
TOM YAM PLA BEUK
GIANT CATFISH IN HOT AND SOUR SOUP

INGREDIENTS

350g giant cat fish or tuna steak

500ml or 2 cups water

1 tsp fresh lime juice, for coating

1 stork lemongrass, cut into 2.5cm lengths

6-8 slices galangal, thinly sliced

2 whole kaffir lime leaves, torn into small pieces

2 fresh red Thai chillies, coarsely crushed

2-3 whole shallots, lightly crushed

1½ tbsp fish sauce

15g sawtooth coriander, cut into 2.5cm length pieces

¾ tbsp fresh lime juice

CHEF'S TIPS

By rubbing freshly squeezed lime juice on the fish; it will help to reduce the fishy smell in the soup stock. Add more fresh chilli if you prefer it more spicy. If so, you should add more of the other ingredients like the fish sauce and lime juice in order to have a well-balanced flavour.

The giant catfish is native to the Mekong River and has a place in the Guinness Book of Records for the largest freshwater fish. It can grow up to 3m and weigh 350kg in the wild. Nowadays the fish meat comes from sustainable farming. Use line caught tuna as a substitute.

METHOD

Sprinkle the lime juice over both sides of the fish and leave it aside.

In a saucepan on a medium to high heat, bring the water to boil and add the lemongrass, galangal, kaffir lime leaves, shallots, chillies and fish sauce. Allow the herbs to infuse for a few minutes.

Bring it to boil rapidly and gently drop in the fish. After 2-3 minutes reduce the heat but make sure the stock is continually boiling and the fish is submerged.

Do not stir at all. Wait until the fish is cooked. This should take another 3-4 minutes depending on the thickness of fish pieces.

Taste. Once satisfied, add the sawtooth coriander and take off the heat immediately.

Pour the soup into a serving bowl which has the fresh lime juice in.

PREPARATION TIME:	COOKING TIME	SERVES	SPICE RATING
10 MINS	10 MINS	2 PEOPLE	

SALADS

Meat, seafood and noodles are the main ingredients in a Thai salad rather than vegetables and salad leaves. These dishes tantalise your taste buds with a balance of flavours, from spiciness, followed by sourness then a hint of saltiness and sweetness at the end. At home these healthy and tasty snacks or starters are also often eaten alongside rice, stir-fries and curries.

ยำเนื้อย่าง

YAM NUA YANG

BARBECUED SIRLOIN STEAK
IN SPICY SALAD WITH CELERY

INGREDIENTS
200g sirloin steak

1 tbsp light soy sauce

Few drops vegetable oil

FOR SALAD

15g Thai celery, cut into 2cm pieces

10g spring onion, cut into 2cm pieces

10g white onion, thinly sliced

2-3 cherry tomatoes, cut in half

FOR SAUCE

1 fresh Thai chilli, coarsely crushed

⅔ tbsp fish sauce

½ tbsp fresh lime juice

¼ tsp sugar

In the summer, barbecue the meat over good quality charcoal to enhance this dish with a smoky flavour.

METHOD

Heat a griddle pan over a very high heat for a few minutes until really hot. Or, if using a grill, heat the oven tray for a few minutes until really hot.

Rub the light soy sauce and oil onto the steak.

Place the steak on a very high heat.

For medium-rare, cook for 2 minutes on each side.

Meanwhile, mix the sauce ingredients together in medium sized bowl.

Make sure all of the sugar is dissolved. Taste and add spice or more lime juice according to your own taste.

Fold all of the salad ingredients into the sauce bowl. Mix well, but gently.

Once the steak is done to your liking, cut into thin slices.

Arrange on a serving dish, pour the salad mix over while the steak is still hot.

Serve.

PREPARATION TIME:	COOKING TIME	SERVES	SPICE RATING
10 MINS	5 MINS	1-2 PEOPLE	

ส้มตำไทย
SOM TAM THAI
GREEN PAPAYA SALAD

The most famous dish from the north east of Thailand. This light, healthy and often spicy salad is now widely available throughout the whole country. It is usually eaten alongside Gai Yang (barbecued chicken) and Kow Neow (sticky rice).

INGREDIENTS

100g unripe green papaya, peeled and shredded

15g carrots, peeled and shredded

1 small clove garlic

1 Thai small red chilli

15g French beans, cut into 2.5cm lengths

3-4 cherry tomatoes, halved

1 tbsp fish sauce

½ tbsp fresh lime juice

2 tsp sugar

1 tbsp unsalted peanuts, whole (optional)

METHOD

Pound the garlic and chilli together coarsely, and preferably with a clay mortar and wooden pestle – these are lighter and more gentle than granite ones.

Add the French beans and roughly pound again.

Add the tomatoes, fish sauce, lime juice and sugar, and gently pound further, just enough to break the tomatoes to mix in with the seasoning.

Add the carrot and papaya.

With the pestle in one hand and a large spoon in the other, lightly pound and mix them, making sure to leave the papaya and carrot still crunchy.

Taste. Add more seasoning if required.

Do not pound again, just use a spoon to get the mix from around the edge of the mortar.

Spoon onto a serving plate and sprinkle the peanuts on top.

Serve.

CHEF'S TIPS

Try to keep the papaya and carrot crunchy by not over pounding it in the mortar and pestle.

PREPARATION TIME:	COOKING TIME	SERVES	SPICE RATING
20-25 MINS	4-5 MINS	1 PERSON	

ยำรวมมิตรทะเล
YAM TALAY
MIXED SEAFOOD SALAD WITH THAI CELERY

INGREDIENTS
4 king prawns, shelled and de-veined
4 pieces squid
2 scallops, cut in half
1 cup water, for poaching
½ tbsp fresh lime juice
¾ tbsp fish sauce
¼ tsp sugar
2 tbsp boiled water
1 fresh Thai chilli, coarsely crushed
1 tbsp white onion, thinly sliced
1 sprig spring onion, cut into 2cm length
2-3 cherry tomatoes, cut in half
Thai celery, cut into 2cm lengths

CHEF'S TIP
The more delicate Thai celery can be substituted with English celery using only the top part near the leaf, cut into 3cm lengths and shred thinly. Use the leaves as well.

This seafood salad is another example of the delicate balance in Thai food, with tangy, spicy, salty and sweet flavours all shining through. If you would like an extra element, you can also add mussels. Alternatively, keep it simple with just squid on its own.

METHOD
In a small bowl, put the fresh lime juice, fish sauce, sugar, boiled water and chilli in. Mix well until sugar has dissolved, then taste.

It should be tangy, followed by spicy and a balance of saltiness with a hint sweetness. Set aside.

In a saucepan, bring water to boil on high heat. Carefully, put in all of the prepared seafood and poach them. This will take 2-3 minutes.

Remove the cooked seafood from the hot water into a mixing bowl. Be very careful not to overcook the seafood as it will shrink and become tough.

Pour the prepared sauce into the cooked seafood bowl. Mix thoroughly and gently fold the onions, tomatoes and celery in.

Serve.

PREPARATION TIME:	COOKING TIME	SERVES	SPICE RATING
15 MINS	5 MINS	2 PEOPLE	

ลาบไก่
LAAB GAI
SPICY MINCED CHICKEN SALAD

A light and healthy dish originating from the north east of Thailand, but extremely popular across the whole country. Try wrapping a spoonful in a crunchy iceberg or gem lettuce leaf.

INGREDIENTS

100g minced chicken breast

½ cup water

¾ tbsp fish sauce

½ tbsp freshly squeezed lime juice

½ tsp sugar

1 tbsp ground roasted rice

¼ tsp roasted dried chilli flakes

50g red onion, finely sliced

25g spring onion, thinly sliced

Small handful mint leaves, finely sliced

TO GARNISH

Mint leaves

CHEF'S TIP

Add the seasoning and red onion while the chicken is still warm. The roasted ground rice should be added at the end so it remains crunchy.

METHOD

Boil the water in a saucepan. Add the minced chicken in and break it up with a ladle, stirring to get it evenly cooked and separated.

This should take about 2 minutes on a high heat.

Remove from heat and immediately add the sugar, fish sauce, chilli and lime juice then mix well.

Add the red onion and again mix thoroughly. The onion will give more sweetness to the salad.

Taste. It should be a balance of tangy and spicy flavours, followed by saltiness with a tiny hint of sweetness. Add more seasoning if required. Once satisfied, add the crunchy ground roasted rice and fold in spring onion and sliced mint leaves.

Serve and garnish with a few fresh mint leaves.

PREPARATION TIME:	COOKING TIME	SERVES	SPICE RATING
10-15 MINS	4-5 MINS	1 PERSON	🌶🌶🌶

ยำส้มโอ
YAM SOM-O

POMELO SALAD WITH SHREDDED CHICKEN AND ROASTED COCONUT FLAKES

INGREDIENTS

80g pomelo

50g chicken in thin flat slices, for shredding

2-3 prawns, de-veined and halved (optional)

1 tbsp coconut flakes, roasted

½ tbsp coconut milk

½ tsp Nam Prik Pow, chilli oil (see page 186)

2 tsp fish sauce

2 tsp sugar

1 fresh lime, juiced

1 cup water

Pomelos grow in abundance in my home town of Prachinburi. Once you get through the thick skin you find something like a refreshing, sweet mild grapefruit. Interestingly the smallest segments are individually sealed and it is possible to eat a whole one without getting juice on your fingers! These individual pieces are the base of this delicious smooth salad.

METHOD

In a shallow pan, roast the coconut flakes on a low heat. Stir really well to get an even, golden brown colour and to release the aroma. Leave it to cool in a small bowl.

Prepare the pomelo by removing the outer and inner white skin completely. Break up the centre of the fruit into the individual pieces and put into a bowl.

In a small saucepan, bring the water to boil and poach the chicken until cooked through.

Remove the cooked chicken pieces from the boiling water and leave to cool.

Immediately, using the same water, poach the prepared prawns. This only takes about 1 minute.

Remove the poached prawns from the water and place into a small bowl. Heat all the seasoning together gently in a small saucepan until the sugar is dissolved, then taste. This salad is a mild one with a more delicate flavoured seasoning.

Check if the chicken is cool then shred them into thin but long pieces. Put them back into the bowl.

Warm the coconut in the same saucepan as before and mix the tasted seasoning in. Take the saucepan off the heat.

Mix the shredded chicken and poached prawns in really well. This is a lukewarm salad.

Fold the pomelo in and place on a serving dish. Sprinkle with the toasted coconut flakes and serve.

PREPARATION TIME:	COOKING TIME	SERVES	SPICE RATING
15 MINS	6-7 MINS	1-2 PEOPLE	🌶🌶🌶

ยำปลาดุกฟู
YAM PLA DUK FOO

CRISPY SEABASS FLAKES WITH SOUR MANGO SALAD

INGREDIENTS
2 seabass fillets

3-4 cups vegetable oil

FOR THE SAUCE
4 tbsp fish sauce

4 tbsp sugar

2 tbsp fresh lime juice

1 fresh Thai chilli, coarsely crushed

FOR THE SALAD
100g sour hard raw mango, shredded

20g red onion, thinly sliced

1 sprig spring onion, thinly cut

10g coriander, coarsely cut

25g unsalted cashew nuts

CHEF'S TIP
Cashew nuts are not one of the main ingredients and can be left out if preferred.

The sour mango in this dish really complements the crispy fish and spicy sauce. If sour mango is not available, use an unripe sweet one instead and increase the lime juice to double the amount. This will achieve the same tangy taste. You can also add or reduce chilli according to your taste.

METHOD
Preheat the grill on a high heat. Place the fish on a baking tray, lining with a piece of foil with the skin side up.

After 6-7 minutes, when the fish is cooked, remove from the heat.

Do not allow the white part to be too brown or dry, if this starts to happen remove from the heat immediately. Leave it to cool.

Alternatively, you can shallow fry the fish in a pan on medium heat, by using two tablespoons of oil and submerging the fish, or turning it to cook evenly until cooked through and golden brown.

Once cooked, leave it to cool.

While the fish is in the grill or frying pan, put all of the sauce ingredients into a saucepan.

On a medium to high heat, bring to the boil, mixing all of the time and being careful not to let it overflow. It will take around 1-2 minutes to achieve a runny syrupy consistency. Take off the heat immediately and leave it to cool.

For the salad, in a small bowl, mix the onions together gently and sprinkle in the cashew nuts and coriander.

Heat the oil in a deep wok or frying pan on very high heat.

Prepare a heatproof bowl by lining with a few pieces of kitchen paper and have two slotted spoons ready to hand.

Using two forks or your hands, remove the white part of cooked fish from the skin and break it all into fine flakes.

When the oil is really hot, gently sprinkle a small amount of the flaky fish each time into the hot oil.

Using the two slotted spoons, submerge the fish or turn it so it is all cooked evenly and so it is golden brown and crispy.

Place into the prepared bowl.

Repeat this process until all fish is crispy fried.

Arrange the crispy fish onto a serving plate.

If eating straight away, put the prepared mango salad on the top and pour the sauce over it.

Alternatively, serve crispy flaked fish, sour mango salad and the spicy syrup sauce in separate bowls and pour over when about to eat.

PREPARATION TIME:	COOKING TIME	SERVES	SPICE RATING
15 MINS	15 MINS	2 PEOPLE	

ปลาซามอลยำใหญ่
SALMON YAM YAI
SALMON SALAD WITH CARAMELISED RED ONION

INGREDIENTS

150g salmon, diced into 3-5cm pieces

50g red onion, thinly sliced

25g ginger, shredded

2 kaffir lime leaves, shredded

25g spring onions, thinly sliced

½ tbsp Nam Prik Pow, chilli oil (see page 186)

½ tbsp fish sauce

1 tsp fresh lime juice

1 tsp sugar

½ tbsp boiled water

1 cup vegetable oil, for frying

There are lots of elements to this tasty salad, but if you'd like to add another, try half a coarse chopped fresh Thai chilli to spice it up.

METHOD
TO MAKE THE SAUCE

Heat a few drops of oil in a shallow frying pan on a medium to high heat.

Sprinkle the red onion in the pan and stir continuously for 1 minute, being careful not to let it stick to the pan.

Turn off the heat and set aside.

In a medium mixing bowl, put in the boiled water, fish sauce, lime juice, chilli oil and sugar. Mix well until the sugar is dissolved.

Add the caramelised red onion and mix again.

To make the salad

In a wok, heat the oil on a high heat. Carefully put the diced salmon in and make sure it is cooked through the middle, and is golden brown evenly, this will take about 3-4 minutes.

Remove the fish onto a piece of kitchen paper then pat the oil off. While it's still hot, put the fried fish into the sauce bowl and mix well. Add ginger, kaffir lime leaves and spring onion. Mix gently and serve.

PREPARATION TIME:	COOKING TIME	SERVES	SPICE RATING
15 MINS	8-10 MINS	2 PEOPLE	

ยำเม็ดมะม่วง
YAM MET MAMMUANG
SALTED CASHEW NUT SALAD

An hors d'oeuvre with a crunch! Perfect alongside pre-dinner drinks.

INGREDIENTS

80g salted cashew nuts

1/8 tsp coarsely crushed red Thai chilli

1 tsp spring onion, finely sliced crossways

¼ tsp fresh lime juice

METHOD

Mix all the ingredients together in a mixing bowl and serve.

PREPARATION TIME:	COOKING TIME	SERVES	SPICE RATING
2 MINS	0 MINS	1 PERSON	

ยำวุ้นเส้นทะเล

YAM WUN SEN TALAY KRATIEM DONG

VERMICELLI SALAD WITH SEAFOOD, MINCED CHICKEN AND PICKLED GARLIC

The pickled garlic is the key to the balance of this dish, adding both a salty and sweet layer to the spiciness of the chilli and tanginess of the fresh lime juice.

INGREDIENTS

60g vermicelli noodles, soaked & cut into 10-12cm lengths

50g chicken, minced

3 king prawns, shelled and de-veined

3 squid pieces

1 cup water, for poaching seafood

FOR SALAD SAUCE

½ tbsp fresh lime juice

⅔ tbsp fish sauce

¼ tsp sugar

2 tbsp boiled water

1 fresh Thai chilli, coarsely crushed

1 tbsp pickled garlic, thinly sliced

1 tbsp red onion, thinly sliced

1 tbsp spring onion, cut into small pieces

2 cherry tomatoes, halved

METHOD

Place the noodles in a bowl and pour over hot water. Leave for 4 minutes, rinse well and using scissors cut into 10-12cm lengths.

In a small bowl, add the pickled garlic, fresh lime juice, fish sauce, sugar and boiled water.

Mix well until sugar has dissolved, then taste. It should be tangy, followed by spicy and a balance of saltiness, with a hint of sweetness.

Please also note that pickled garlic has saltiness and sweetness in it, so it is best to not over season with fish sauce or sugar

Once satisfied leave it aside.

In a saucepan, bring the water to boil.

Poach all the prepared seafood for approximately 2-3 minutes.

Remove the cooked seafood from the hot water and place into a bowl.

Add 2-3 tablespoons of water to the saucepan, bring it to boil and add minced chicken.

Using a wooden spoon, quickly separate and do not allow the chicken to form into big pieces. It should take very little time for the chicken to cook.

Add a few drops of water if it's dry, then add vermicelli noodles.

Stir the noodles in the cooked chicken quickly.

Fold the noodles in until cooked, which shouldn't take long at all. Remove it from the heat immediately. Drain some juice away to leave only about a spoonful.

If the noodles stick together into a big clump, do not try to separate them.

Pour the prepared sauce into the cooked noodles, using a wooden spoon to fold them into the sauce quickly.

This will help to separate the noodles, but be careful not to break them into small pieces.

Add poached seafood, onions and tomatoes.

Mix well and serve.

PREPARATION TIME:	COOKING TIME	SERVES	SPICE RATING
20 MINS	5 MINS	1-2 PEOPLE	🌶🌶🌶

ปลาซามอลดิบกับยำตะไคร้
PLA SALMON
SALMON SASHIMI WITH LEMONGRASS SALAD

INGREDIENTS

60g sashimi grade salmon loin, thinly sliced

1 tbsp lemongrass, finely sliced

1 tbsp ginger, shredded lengthways

1 tbsp spring onions, thinly sliced

1 tbsp red onion or shallots, thinly sliced

1-2 kaffir lime leaves

¼-½ tbsp freshly squeezed lime juice

1 tsp sugar

3-4 mint leaves

1½ tbsp Nam Prik Pow, chilli oil (see page 186)

1 fresh small chilli, finely chopped (optional)

CHEF'S TIP

Always use the best grade salmon for this uncooked salmon dish.

This salad greatly benefits if you make it as fresh as possible. Chop the salad ingredients shortly before mixing them to ensure the best flavours shine through.

METHOD

Mix all of the ingredients together except the fresh chilli.

Taste, and add the fresh chilli if required.

Place the salad on the serving plate with the thinly sliced salmon on the top or to the side.

PREPARATION TIME:	COOKING TIME	SERVES	SPICE RATING
10-15 MINS	0 MINS	1 PERSON	🌶🌶🌶

MEAT

I have fond memories of the wonderful aromas emanating from Moo Pa Loa bubbling away in the kitchen, being one of the slow cooked meat dishes these would tantalisingly drift around the house for hours before the meal was ready. Stir-fries on the other hand are quick cooking with more time spent on the preparation of ingredients.

เนื้อสวรรค์
NUA SAWAN

HEAVENLY BEEF

INGREDIENTS

300g rump steak, thinly sliced

50ml oyster sauce

40g sugar

10g coriander seeds, coarsely ground

TO GARNISH

Holy basil leaves

2 cups cooking oil

This dish lives up to its name!

METHOD

Put all the ingredients in a mixing bowl. Mix by hand thoroughly. Cover and leave to marinate overnight.

TO SERVE

Heat the oil in a wok on high heat. Meanwhile, line a bowl with some pieces of kitchen paper.

Drop the holy basil leaves in the hot oil and use a slatted spoon to submerge all of the leaves, then immediately remove them from the hot oil.

Drain on to the prepared kitchen paper.

This process will take less than 30 seconds. The leaves will turn brown if left for too long in the hot oil.

Prepare a fine sieve with a heatproof bowl. Drain the oil into it to remove any crumb from crispy basil leaves.

Put the oil back in the wok. Fry the beef in the hot oil on a high heat, stirring all the time to ensure the beef is cooked evenly. This will take 4-5 minutes.

Remove from the oil and serve on a warm plate. Arrange the crispy basil leaves nicely on top.

PREPARATION TIME: 15MINS PLUS TIME TO MARINATE OVERNIGHT	COOKING TIME 6-7 MINS	SERVES 2-3 PEOPLE	SPICE RATING 🌶🌶🌶

หมูทอดกระเทียมพริกไท
MOO TOD KRATIAM PRIK THAI

PORK WITH GARLIC AND BLACK PEPPER

A simple and delicious way of cooking pork loin. Perfect with some sticky white rice.

INGREDIENTS

150g pork loin, thinly sliced

2 tbsp vegetable oil

1-2 cloves garlic, coarsely chopped

½ tsp black pepper, coarsely ground

1 tbsp oyster sauce

¼ tsp sugar

1-2 tbsp water

TO GARNISH

1 tsp Kratiem Grob, crispy fried garlic (see page 186)

METHOD

Put the oil in a wok on a medium heat.

Add the chopped garlic in and stir until the aroma is released.

Put the prepared pork in and turn the heat up to high. Stir for a few minutes and add the black pepper.

Continue stirring for half a minute more. Add the oyster sauce, sugar and water, a little at a time.

Mix really well until the pork is cooked. Taste and add more seasoning or water if necessary.

Serve on a warm plate.

Sprinkle the crispy garlic flakes over the top.

PREPARATION TIME:	COOKING TIME	SERVES	SPICE RATING
20MINS	7-8 MINS	2 PEOPLE	🌶🌶🌶

เนื้อผัดน้ำมันหอยกับหน่อไม้ฝรั่ง
NUA PAD NAMAN HOY NORMAI FARANG

BEEF STIR-FRY IN OYSTER SAUCE WITH ASPARAGUS

INGREDIENTS
120g rump steak, fat removed and thinly sliced

1 bunch asparagus

2 tbsp vegetable oil

1 small clove garlic, coarsely chopped

1 tbsp oyster sauce

¼ tsp sugar

½ cup water, for blanching

CHEF'S TIPS
This tasty stir-fry relies on precise cooking times and techniques for the perfect texture. The asparagus must be blanched (cooking for a couple of minutes in boiling water, then plunged into cold water) otherwise it will become soggy. Avoid over cooking the thinly sliced beef by only keeping it on the heat for a couple of minutes.

This dish contains no chilli, so it is perfect for balancing a meal alongside spicier dishes, on its own when no spice is preferred.

METHOD
In a saucepan, on a high heat, bring the water to boil. Blanch asparagus for 1-2 minutes.

Drain the water off and arrange onto a warm serving plate.

Heat the oil in a wok on a medium heat. Put the garlic in, stir to release the aroma and turn golden brown, being careful not to let it burn.

Immediately put the steak in and turn up the heat to high.

Add the oyster sauce and sugar, stirring continuously for no longer than 2 minutes, adding a little water if more sauce is required.

Arrange the beef stir-fry on top of the asparagus.

Serve immediately.

PREPARATION TIME:	COOKING TIME	SERVES	SPICE RATING
8-10 MINS	4-5 MINS	1 PERSON	

ไก่ผัดเม็ดมะม่วงหิมพานต์
GAI PAD MET MAMMUANG

STIR-FRIED CHICKEN WITH CASHEW NUTS AND DRIED CHILLI

INGREDIENTS

160g chicken breast, thinly sliced

2 tbsp vegetable oil

1 small clove garlic, coarsely chopped

1 tbsp oyster sauce

¼ tsp sugar

2 tbsp water

1 small handful white onion, thinly sliced

1 sprig spring onion, cut into 1.5cm lengths

Small handful unsalted cashew nuts

1 large dried chilli, cut into 1.5cm pieces

CHEF'S TIPS

The onions should only be lightly cooked to add an extra layer of texture, flavour and freshness.

The flavoursome roasted dried chilli is the star of this stir-fry.

METHOD

To roast the chilli, add a few drops of oil to a wok on a low to medium heat, add the dried chilli and stir to release the aroma.

The oil will lightly coat the chilli and give it a slightly crispy texture.

The oil should not be so deep as to fry it.

This procedure produces very stong fumes and should always be done in a well ventilated area. Do not breathe in the fumes.

Once the aroma is released, remove from the heat and leave in a bowl to cool.

Heat a wok on a medium heat and add the rest of the vegetable oil.

Put the garlic in and stir to release the aroma, just for a few seconds.

Add the chicken and turn the heat up to high. Stir vigorously for 2-3 minutes, until almost cooked.

Add the oyster sauce, sugar and half of the water first, adding more as necessary to make a gravy. Taste and season further, if required.

Gently stir in all of the onion for 30 seconds. Turn off the heat and sprinkle the cashew nuts and dried chillies on top.

Serve.

PREPARATION TIME:	COOKING TIME	SERVES	SPICE RATING
10 MINS	4-5 MINS	1-2 PEOPLE	🌶🌶🌶

ไก่ผัดพริกแกงเขียวหวานแห้ง
GAI PAD KEO WAN HAENG
CHICKEN STIR-FRY IN DRY GREEN CURRY PASTE WITH PEA AUBERGINES

INGREDIENTS

150g chicken breast, thinly sliced

2 tbsp vegetable oil

2 tbsp Kreuang Gaeng Keo Wan, green curry paste (see page 184)

1 tbsp sugar

2 tbsp coconut milk

3-4 tbsp water

15g pea aubergines

2 kaffir lime leaves, whole

Small handful sweet basil leaves

Few pieces long red chilli, cut diagonally

A stir-fry with all of the ingredients of a green curry. A great alternative with a more concentrated flavour than the sauce based one.

METHOD

Put the oil in a wok on medium heat. Add the curry paste and stir vigorously.

Quickly add coconut milk to stop it sticking to the pan and add some water to keep it wet. Once the aroma is released, add the chicken and stir thoroughly.

Make sure the chicken is thoroughly coated with curry paste and then add the pea aubergines.

Stir for about 3-4 minutes until the chicken is cooked, then add the sugar.

Add a little more water if required.

Mix in the chilli and kaffir lime leaves and continue to cook for a further minute.

Turn the heat off and gently fold in the sweet basil leaves.

Serve.

PREPARATION TIME:
15 MINS PLUS TIME TO CREATE THE PASTE

COOKING TIME
7 MINS

SERVES
2 PEOPLE

SPICE RATING

หมูพะโล้
MOO PALOA

SLOW COOKED PORK BELLY WITH CINNAMON AND STAR ANISE

This is a deliciously fragrant dish with tender pork and herby gravy. You can add a few hard boiled eggs if desired, simply make sure they are all submerged to get an even colour about five minutes before finishing time.

INGREDIENTS

1kg lean belly pork, cut into 3-4 pieces
4-5 cinnamon sticks
½ tsp cinnamon powder
4-5 star anise
4 whole pickled garlic bulbs
3-4 whole garlic cloves
1 tsp whole black peppercorns
25g coriander roots, lightly pounded
2-3 tbsp oyster sauce
1-2 tbsp light soy sauce
1-2 tsp dark soy sauce
1 tbsp vegetable oil
60g palm sugar
1½ litres water

CHEF'S TIPS

Ask the butcher for the leanest piece possible, with only a tiny layer of fat between the pork skin and flesh.

The sugar should only be added once the pork is tender.

METHOD

Preheat the oven to 150-160°c.

In a heavy casserole dish, heat the oil on a medium heat.

Put all the herbs and sauces in except for the sugar, and stir for about 2-3 minutes, until the aroma is released.

Add the pork belly with skin facing up and immediately add water.

Make sure all of the pork pieces are submerged.

Turn the heat up, bring it to boil and leave for a few minutes.

Remove any dark foam floating on the top and put a lid on.

When the oven is hot and ready, place this casserole dish on the bottom shelf of a hot oven.

Leave it swimming in the oven for 1½ hours.

Check the pork belly tenderness with a small sharp knife – be very careful touching the lid as it will be extremely hot.

Taste the gravy at this point and add more seasoning if required, but do not add the sugar yet.

Put it back in the oven if the meat is not tender enough.

Once the pork flesh is soft, add the sugar for the last few minutes.

Stir on the hob until the sugar is dissolved or put the casserole dish back into the oven for a further few minutes.

Taste. If satisfied, divide and serve hot.

PREPARATION TIME:	COOKING TIME	SERVES	SPICE RATING
20 MINS	1½-2 HOURS	3-4 PEOPLE	🌶🌶🌶

ไก่ย่าง
GAI YANG
BARBECUED CHICKEN

Gai Yang is one of the most popular everyday meals in Thailand, along with Som Tam Thai (green papaya salad) and Kow Neow (sticky rice).

INGREDIENTS

1.5kg (approx) whole chicken, cleaned

10g coriander seeds, finely ground

10g garlic

10g fresh coriander root or stork, finely cut

A few finely ground black peppercorns

50g sugar

1 tbsp oyster sauce

1 tbsp light soy sauce

1 tsp dark soy sauce

1 tbsp vegetable oil

2 tbsp coconut milk, thickest part

CHEF'S TIP

This is is often eaten with green papaya salad and sticky rice, however if you would like to eat it alone, serve with spicy roasted chilli flake sauce.

METHOD
TO MARINATE

Cut the chicken in half down the breast.

Make two or three diagonal cuts onto any thick part of the chicken so that the flavour can be absorbed and to ensure it cooks through easily.

Wash, drain and pat dry with kitchen paper.

Place in a large mixing bowl and set aside.

To prepare the marinade, put the garlic and coriander into a heavy mortar and pestle and pound them until very fine.

Add the ground coriander seeds, ground black peppercorns and sugar, and pound again.

Add into the bowl with the chicken, along the rest of the ingredients.

Mix them together by hand (using disposable gloves if preferred). Make sure all of the herbs and seasoning coat every part of the chicken. Cover and leave this to marinate for at least 2 hours, or preferably overnight.

TO GRILL OR BARBECUE

Preheat the grill to maximum heat.

Put all of the marinated chicken on an oven tray, with the skin facing down.

Cook for 25 minutes.

Turn over and continue cooking for a further 20-25 minutes, until the chicken is cooked and the skin is quite brown.

Check the thickest part of the chicken with a sharp knife. If cooked, the juices that run out will be clear.

Alternatively, barbecue over charcoal for a smoky flavour.

PREPARATION TIME:	COOKING TIME	SERVES	SPICE RATING
15-20 MINS, PLUS MARINATE OVERNIGHT	40-50 MINUTES	4-5 PEOPLE	

CURRIES

Thai curries are made up from curry paste and coconut milk, meat, seafood and vegetables. The different curry pastes all contain chilli, and a mixture of fresh and dried herbs and spices, all ground into a paste in the ubiquitous mortar and pestle. In the case of red and green curry the name refers to the colour of the chillies used to make the paste. Fiery 'Jungle' curry is the exception as it is stock based with no coconut milk.

แกงเขียวปลาใส่ผักชีลาว

GAENG KEO WAN PLA PAK CHEE LAO

COD LOIN IN GREEN CURRY WITH DILL

INGREDIENTS

200g cod loin

FOR THE SAUCE

1½ tbsp Kreuang Gaeng Keo Wan, green curry paste (see page 184)

1 tin coconut milk

1 tbsp vegetable oil

1 tsp fish sauce

½ tsp sugar

1 tbsp small pieces dill, removed from stem

1-2 cups water

TO GARNISH

1 small sprig dill

CHEF'S TIP

Check the fish often, taking care not to scald yourself when removing the steamer's lid. Take it out the instant a thin-bladed knife meets no resistance when poking the flesh.

The dill in this dish adds another dimension to the classic Thai green curry.

METHOD

Put at least 2.5cm of water in the bottom of a steamer, cover and bring to a boil over high heat.

Lay the fish on the steamer's rack, making sure the rack is elevated above the water, and cover again. Steam for 6-8 minutes, or until the fish is done. When ready, serve in a warm bowl.

Meanwhile, heat the oil and curry paste in a wok on a medium to high heat. Stir continuously for about 1-2 minutes.

Add a few spoonfuls of coconut milk to make a wet paste.

Turn the heat down to medium and stir for a few minutes until the aroma is released.

Add the rest of coconut milk, and mix well.

Add fish sauce and sugar. If the sauce is too thick, add half of the water first. Add more if required, stirring all the time.

Once you achieve the right consistency, leave the curry sauce boiling gently for a few minutes. Sprinkle the dill in.

Pour the green curry sauce over the steamed fish and garnish with a sprig of dill.

PREPARATION TIME:	COOKING TIME	SERVES	SPICE RATING
10 MINS PLUS TIME TO MAKE THE PASTE	8 MINS	1-2 PEOPLE	🌶🌶🌶

แพนงเนื้อย่าง

PENANG NUA YANG

FILLET STEAK WITH RICH 'PENANG' CURRY

This rich and flavoursome dish can be served in its own right with steamed Thai fragrant rice, or eaten as part of a communal meal along with a selection of salad, stir-fry vegetables and rice.

INGREDIENTS

200-250g fillet steak, about 2½cm thick

2 tsp vegetable oil

2 tbsp Keuang Gaeng Paneang, paneang curry paste (see page 185)

1 tin coconut milk

2 tbsp sugar

2 tbsp fish sauce

TO GARNISH

2 kaffir lime leaves, cut into fine strips

1 red chilli, sliced

METHOD

Heat the oil in a wok on medium heat and fry the curry paste, breaking it up to release the aroma.

Add 4 tablespoons of the thicker part of the coconut milk and stir. When you see dots of oil floating on the top, add the rest of the coconut milk and the seasoning.

Simmer over a medium heat until the sauce is reduced by almost half.

Taste and season again if necessary.

Meanwhile, preheat the grill on maximum and grill the fillet steak to your preference.

When the steak is done, slice into 1-2cm slices, arrange on a warm serving plate and pour the curry over.

Sprinkle with the kaffir lime leaves and sliced chilli.

CHEF'S TIPS

Penang curry sauce is thicker and has a stronger flavour than green curry.

Grill the steak whilst the sauce is simmering.

PREPARATION TIME:	COOKING TIME	SERVES	SPICE RATING
10 MINS PLUS TIME TO MAKE THE PASTE	8 MINS	2 PEOPLE	

GAENG PED BET YANG

HONEY ROASTED DUCK IN
RED CURRY WITH RAMBUTANS

INGREDIENTS

FOR MARINADE

250g duck breast

2-3 tbsp unset honey

1 tbsp light soy sauce

FOR CURRY SAUCE

2 tbsp Kreuang Gaeng Daeng, red curry paste (see page 184)

1 tin coconut milk

1 tbsp vegetable oil

½ tsp sugar

½-¾ cup water

TO GARNISH

2-3 rambutans in syrup

1 cherry tomato, cut in half

2 whole kaffir lime leaves

Another example of a savoury dish with tropical fruit. My home town of Prachinburi is renowned for fruit growing, especially rambutans, which are in the same family as lychees.

METHOD

Marinate the duck breast by rubbing the honey and soy sauce onto the breast in a small bowl. Cover it and leave it for a minimum of 2 hours, preferably overnight if you have time.

Preheat the oven to about 200-220°c. Place the marinated duck onto the baking tray with the skin down.

After 7 minutes, turn it over.

After another 8 minutes the skin should be golden brown and the breast should be a very light pink in the middle. Adjust the roasting time according to the thickness of the duck breast.

Leave it to cool before slicing into pieces about 1cm thick.

WHILE ROASTING THE DUCK, PREPARE THE CURRY SAUCE.

In a wok on a medium to high heat, put the oil and curry paste in. Stir continuously for about 1 minute. Add 3-4 spoonfuls from the thick part of the coconut milk to make a wet paste.

Turn the heat down to medium, stir for a few minutes until the aroma is released and there are a few dots of oil floating on the top.

Add the rest of the coconut milk and bring to the boil.

Add sugar. If the sauce is too thick, add half of the water first. Add more if required, stirring all the time.

Once you achieve the right consistency, add the sliced roasted duck and cook for about 1-2 minutes. Remove from the heat. Pour into a warm serving bowl. Drop in the cherry tomato, kaffir lime leaves and a few rambutans.

Serve.

PREPARATION TIME:	COOKING TIME	SERVES	SPICE RATING
10 MINS MARINADE FOR AT LEAST 2 HOURS	20 MINS	2 PEOPLE	

GAENG KEO WAN GAI
GREEN CURRY WITH CHICKEN

INGREDIENTS

180g chicken breast, thinly sliced

4 wedges eggplant or Thai aubergines (optional)

50g bamboo shoots, drained

Small handful sweet basil leaves

1½ tbsp Kreuang Gaeng Keo Wan, green curry paste, (see page 184)

1 tin coconut milk

Tiny pinch turmeric powder

1 tbsp vegetable oil

½ tsp fish sauce

1½ tsp sugar

1 kaffir lime leaf

1-2 cups water

TO GARNISH

Long red chilli, finely stripped

Small sprig of sweet basil

This is one of the most well known Thai dishes. Eat simply with steamed rice or alongside a well balanced selection of dishes to share. Green curry sauce is slightly sweeter than its red cousin, use more or less curry paste according to your taste.

METHOD

Heat the oil in a wok on high heat and stir in the curry paste.

Add turmeric powder and a few spoonfuls of coconut milk to make a wet paste.

Turn the heat down to medium and stir for a few minutes until the aroma is released and there are a few dots of oil floating on the top.

Add the rest of the coconut milk, turn the heat up and add the kaffir lime leaf, fish sauce and sugar.

If the sauce is too thick, add half of the water first. And add more if required, stirring all the time. Once you achieve the right consistency, leave the curry sauce boiling gently for a few minutes.

With the heat on full, bring the sauce to boil and add the sliced chicken, bamboo shoots and eggplant/aubergine wedges.

Stir and mix until the chicken is cooked. This will take about 4-5 minutes.

Gently mix the basil leaves in. Remove from the heat and serve in a warm bowl. Garnish with strips of long red chilli and sweet basil leaves.

PREPARATION TIME:	COOKING TIME	SERVES	SPICE RATING
10 MINS PLUS TIME TO MAKE THE PASTE	10 MINS	2 PEOPLE	

GAENG PA GAI

'JUNGLE CURRY' WITH
FRESH PEPPERCORNS AND CHICKEN

INGREDIENTS

150g chicken, thinly sliced

2 tbsp Kreuang Gaeng Daeng, red curry paste, (see page 184)

2 cups water

½ tsp fish sauce

¼ tsp sugar

15g Thai aubergines, cut into quarters

15g pea aubergines

2 kaffir lime leaves

10g krachai, shredded

15g fresh green beans, cut into 4cm lengths

25g bamboo shoots strips

Fresh peppercorn, cut to 2cm lengths

15g long red chilli, sliced diagonally

Small handful holy basil leaves

This is the hottest of the curries with the distinctive taste of krachai, an aromatic vegetable from the ginger family. Jungle curry is a stock based curry and therefore does not contain coconut milk. If you'd like it even spicier, add a coarsely chopped small Thai chilli and try to get a peppercorn in each spoonful when eating!

METHOD

In a wok on medium high heat, put in one cup of water and the curry paste.

Stir and break up the curry paste until it is well mixed.

Add the rest of the water and bring it to boil.

Add the chicken and Thai aubergines at the same time, as they will take a few minutes to cook.

Season with the fish sauce and sugar and stir before adding the krachai.

Bring the heat down to medium to allow the krachai to infuse the dish with flavour until the chicken is cooked. Add the fresh peppercorns, green beans and bamboo shoots.

Taste. Add more water or seasoning if required.

Once satisfied, drop the chilli in and mix.

Turn the heat off and gently fold in the holy basil leaves.

Serve immediately.

PREPARATION TIME:	COOKING TIME	SERVES	SPICE RATING
15 MINS PLUS TIME TO MAKE THE PASTE	7-8 MINS	1-2 PEOPLE	🌶🌶🌶

แกงมัสหมันเนือ

GAENG MASSAMAN NUA
MASSAMAN BEEF CURRY

The very popular Massaman Curry originates from the south of Thailand.

INGREDIENTS

250g braising steak cut into about 5cm cubes

½ cup water

100ml coconut milk, thin part

½ tbsp peanut halves

6-7 baby potatoes

2-3 shallots, peeled

FOR THE CURRY SAUCE

300ml coconut milk thick part

2 tbsp Kreuang Gaeng Massaman, massaman curry paste (see page 185)

1 tsp fish sauce

2 tsp sugar

1 tbsp tamarind juice

½ cup water

TO GARNISH

Hom Jeow, crispy fried shallots (see page 187)

CHEF'S TIP

Alternatively, use cubed chicken or chicken drumsticks instead of cubed braising steak. The tenderising time will be shorter, even with same amount of meat.

METHOD
FOR THE MEAT

Bring the water and coconut milk to the boil in a saucepan.
Put the steak in and bring it to the boil for about 10 minutes.
Reduce the heat down to medium and continue simmering the cubed steak for 1 hour. Add the peanuts to the simmering steaks and continue simmering on medium heat for about 30 minutes, or until both the peanuts and the cubed steak are tender.
Drain all of the juice away in a colander when they are done.
Whilst the steak is simmering, if you are going to do your own curry paste, this is the time to start. See page 185 for recipe.
Peel and wash the potatoes, Then boil them for about 10 minutes or until just cooked through. Rinse with cool tap water and leave them aside.

FOR THE CURRY SAUCE

Peel the shallots and leave them in a small bowl.
To make the curry sauce, heat the oil and curry paste in a wok on a medium to high heat.
Stir and add a few spoonfuls of coconut milk to make a wet paste. Stir vigorously for 1-2 minutes, until the aroma is released.
Turn the heat down to medium and stir continuously for about 2-3 minutes more. There should be a few dots of oil floating on the top. Then add the rest of coconut milk and mix well.
Put the shallots in and add the fish sauce, sugar and tamarind juice. Check if the sauce is too thick, add half of the water first, then add more later if required.
Leave the curry sauce boiling gently for about 5-6 minutes until the shallots are done. It should be slightly thicker than the normal red or green curry.
Leave it aside and add the tendered steak and peanuts in while they are hot.
Simmer gently on a medium heat for about 4-5 minutes.
Ensure that all of the steak and potatoes are covered with the curry sauce while simmering.
Add more water and quickly bring it to the boil. Or, add hot boiled water. Mix well to achieve the consistency required.
Taste. This should be a mild, sweet curry with a hint of sourness from tamarind juice.
Serve hot and sprinkle a tablespoonful of crispy fried shallots on the top

---

PREPARATION TIME:	COOKING TIME	SERVES	SPICE RATING
20 MINS PLUS TIME TO MAKE THE PASTE	1½ HOURS	2 PEOPLE	

แกงกะหรีไก่

GAENG KARI GAI

CHICKEN AND SWEET POTATO YELLOW CURRY

My mother always used chicken drumsticks or portions as Thai people prefer the darker meat of chicken. This curry is perfect for that.

INGREDIENTS

180g chicken breast, cut into 8-10 cubed pieces (alternatively use chicken drumsticks or chicken portions)

1½-2 tbsp Kreuang Gaeng Kari, yellow curry paste (see page 185)

½ tbsp vegetable oil

250ml coconut milk

100g sweet potatoes, cut into about 3cm cubed pieces

60g white onions, cut into 3cm pieces

2 tsp sugar

2 tsp fish sauce

¼-½ cup water

METHOD

In a saucepan on a high heat, put the oil and curry paste in. Stir for 30 seconds and add 3-4 tablespoons of the thick part of the coconut milk.

Mix well for about 2 minutes, until the aroma is released.

Put the cubes of chicken in the wet paste and reduce the heat slightly.

Cook and turn for about 4-5 minutes, until the outer layer of the chicken pieces change colour.

Turn the heat up and quickly add the rest of the coconut milk and onion.

Put half of the water in first, then add the sweet potatoes and bring it to boil.

Then season with one tablespoon of fish sauce and sugar.

Mix well and add more water or more coconut milk if required. Once satisfied with the curry sauce consistency, taste.

Add more seasoning if required. This curry should be nicely balanced between spicy, saltiness and sweetness.

After 6-8 minutes, the potatoes should be cooked.

The potatoes will take different times to cook, depending on the size. If they are cut into small pieces, less time is required to cook. Be careful not to overcook them, as they will be mushy.

Serve hot.

PREPARATION TIME:	COOKING TIME	SERVES	SPICE RATING
10 - 15 MINS PLUS TIME TO MAKE THE PASTE	13-15 MINS	2 PEOPLE	

แกงเหลืองใต้ปลากับสัปรส

GAENG LEUANG PLA PAKTAI

SOUTHERN SOUR YELLOW CURRY

WITH PINEAPPLE AND SILVER HAKE STEAK

INGREDIENTS

200g silver hake steak

½ tsp fresh lime juice

1½ tbsp Kreuang Gaeng Kari, yellow curry paste (see page 185)

100g fresh under ripe pineapple, cut into ½cm thick and 2cm width chunks

1 tbsp fish sauce

1 tsp sugar

1 tbsp Nam Makarm Piek, tamarind juice (see page 186)

400ml water

CHEF'S TIP

The amount of sugar and tamarind juice you use is dictated by how ripe the pineapple is. If possible avoid using a very ripe one.

If the pineapple is sweet, reduce the sugar and vice versa; if it is sour reduce the tamarind juice slightly.

For an alternative, unripe papaya or pickled bamboo shoots can be used instead of pineapple.

Adjust the seasoning according to the nature of the vegetable used.

Fresh fish is important for this curry, as is the balance of flavours. See the chef's tip for ways to make sure the dish is not overly sweet or too sour.

METHOD

Cut the fish into two pieces and rub the fresh lime juice on both sides.

This will stop any fishy smell and will help it to keep its shape when cooking. Leave until ready to cook.

In a deep saucepan, bring the water to boil on a high heat and add the curry paste.

Stir to mix the curry paste in and add the pineapple. Boil the pineapple for a few minutes to release its flavour.

Gently put the fish in and submerge in the curry sauce. Do not stir as this will create a fishy smell and the stock will become cloudy.

Season with half of the fish sauce at first and add the tamarind juice and all of the sugar.

Leave them to cook for around 3-4 minutes.

When you can see the fish begin to curl up and shrink a little, turn or stir gently to ensure all of the fish has been submerged and leave for a further 3-4 minutes.

Taste and add the rest of fish sauce if required.

Serve immediately.

PREPARATION TIME:	COOKING TIME	SERVES	SPICE RATING
10 MINS PLUS TIME TO MAKE THE PASTE	7-8 MINS	2 PEOPLE	♨♨♨

SEAFOOD

Thailand has an extensive coastline and many islands. As a result, the seafood industry is thriving. The best way to enjoy it is at an open air restaurant, in a fishing village looking out at the brightly coloured fishing boats plying the azure sea. Here the daily catch can be enjoyed just minutes after being brought to shore.

ปลาดุกทอดกระเทียมพริกไทย
PLA DUK TOD KRATIEM PRIK THAI

PANGUS WITH GARLIC AND BLACK PEPPER SAUCE
TOPPED WITH CRISPY GARLIC FLAKES

This dish is a real delight to cook, the aroma from the garlic, black pepper and kaffir lime leaves will get your taste buds tingling.

INGREDIENTS

300g pangus, cut into 5-6 large pieces

3 cups vegetable oil

2 cloves garlic, coarsely chopped

1 tsp black pepper, coarsely ground

1 tbsp oyster sauce

¼ tsp sugar

2-3 tbsp water

3-4 whole kaffir lime leaves

1 tbsp Kratiem Grob, crispy fried garlic (see page 186)

METHOD

Prepare a heatproof tray with a few pieces of kitchen paper lining.

Heat the oil in a deep wok on a high heat.

Drop the kaffir lime leaves in for a few seconds only, until you can see them turn translucent.

Remove them from the hot oil onto the prepared tray then put them aside in a little bowl.

Fry the prepared fish in the hot oil for about 4-5 minutes or until light golden brown, just to get some parts crispy.

Remove the fried fish onto a plate with a few pieces of kitchen paper lining.

Reduce the heat to quite low.

Remove most of the hot oil, leaving only one tablespoon in the wok.

Put the chopped garlic in and stir on a low heat until the aroma is released, then add black pepper.

Continue stirring for a further 30 seconds.

Turn up the heat and add oyster sauce, sugar and water.

Mix really well and check the consistency. The sauce should be of a medium thickness.

Taste, add more water if necessary and bring to boil.

Turn off the heat.

Arrange the fried fish on a warm serving plate. Pour the sauce gently onto the fish. Sprinkle with crispy kaffir lime leaves and the crispy garlic flakes.

Serve.

PREPARATION TIME:	COOKING TIME	SERVES	SPICE RATING
20 MINS	10 MINS	2 PEOPLE	🌶🌶🌶

ปลาทูน่าทอดกระเทียมพริกไทย
TUNA NEUNG RAAD KRATIAM PRIKTHAI

STEAMED TUNA WITH GARLIC AND BLACK PEPPER SAUCE

INGREDIENTS

200g tuna steak

1 tbsp vegetable oil

2 cloves garlic, coarsely chopped

1 tsp pepper, coarsely ground

1½ tbsp oyster sauce

¼ tsp sugar

2-3 tbsp water

TO GARNISH

1 tbsp Kratiem Grob, crispy fried garlic (see page 186)

The crispy garlic flakes really are the icing on the cake of this delicious tuna dish.

METHOD

Pat dry the tuna steak and leave it at room temperature for 5-6 minutes.

Put at least 3cm of water in the bottom of a steamer, cover and bring to boil over a high heat.

Lay the fish on the steaming rack, making sure the rack is elevated above the water, and cover again. Steam for 5-6 minutes, or until the fish is done.

Meanwhile, prepare the garlic and pepper sauce. Heat the oil in a wok on medium to high heat.

Fry the garlic until the aroma is released and add the black pepper. Stir for half a minute and then quickly add the oyster sauce, sugar and water.

Mix really well and check the consistency. This should be a slightly thick sauce.

Remove the cooked tuna from the steamer and place in the wok, into the garlic and black pepper sauce.

Reduce the heat slightly and spoon the sauce over to cover the steak. Cook for half a minute further.

Serve the fish on a warm serving plate. Sprinkle a spoonful of crispy garlic flakes over to garnish.

Serve.

PREPARATION TIME:	COOKING TIME	SERVES	SPICE RATING
15 MINS	6-7 MINS	1 PERSON	

ปลานึงมะนาว
PLA NEUNG MENOW
STEAMED SEA BASS WITH LIME AND CHILLI

Lime and chilli are classic and simple ingredients in Thai cooking that easily complement most dishes, although they are particularly good with a fish as meaty as sea bass.

INGREDIENTS

2 fillets or 225-250g sea bass, skin on, scaled, pin bones removed

¼ cup water

FOR THE LIME AND CHILLI SAUCE

10g Thai chillies, whole

7g or 2 garlic cloves, whole and peeled

5g coriander, root or storks finely cut

1 ½ tbsp fish sauce

1 tbsp fresh lime juice

2 tsp sugar

2 tbsp boiled water

TO GARNISH

1 fresh lime, thinly sliced

1 spring onion, cut into 4cm lengths

METHOD

Put at least 5cm of water in the bottom of a steamer, cover and bring to a boil over high heat.

Lay the fish fillets together. The fillet on the bottom should have the skin facing down and the fillet on the top should have the skin facing up.

Place the bowl on the steamer trivet, cover and steam on medium heat for 10-12 minutes.

While steaming the fish, coarsely chop the chilli and garlic together and add finely cut coriander. Chop them together and mix well.

Put it in a small saucepan with the remaining seasoning and boiled water.

Bring to a gentle boil to dissolve the sugar.

Do not leave it boil for too long – the garlic and chilli needs to be cooked without releasing too much of a garlic flavour.

Taste. The sauce should be tangy, spicy at first with a good balance of saltiness and a hint of sweetness. Add more seasoning if required.

When satisfied, add the spring onion.

Remove from the heat immediately, but keep warm.

When the fish is cooked, transfer the fish and stock into a warm serving bowl.

Lay the slices of limes on the top.

Pour the warm lime chilli sauce over the hot fish and serve immediately.

PREPARATION TIME:	COOKING TIME	SERVES	SPICE RATING
10 MINS	12-15 MINS	2 PEOPLE	

ปลานึงขิง
PLA NEUNG KING
STEAMED SEA BASS WITH GINGER AND SPRING ONION

This dish is healthy, flavoursome, fragrant and quick to make. A real winner.

INGREDIENTS

225-250g or 2 fillets sea bass, skin on, scaled, pin bones removed

¼ cup water

1 tbsp light soy sauce

10g ginger, thinly sliced

2 cloves garlic, thinly sliced

TO GARNISH

1 handful spring onion, thinly shredded into 5-7cm long pieces.

Soak in cool water in a deep small bowl for 10 minutes and drain.

METHOD

Put at least 5cm of water in the bottom of a steamer, cover and bring to a boil over high heat.

In a shallow bowl, lay one fillet with the skin down. Place a few pieces of ginger and garlic on the fillet. Then lay the other fillet fish with the skins outside on the top. Scatter the rest of the ginger and garlic on top.

Add the soy sauce and water.

Place the bowl on the steamer's rack making sure it is elevated above the water.

Cover and steam on medium heat for 10-12 minutes. Check if the fish is cooked.

Taste. It is fine to add more soy sauce if required, or add a drop of boiling water if it is too strong in flavour at this stage.

Transfer the fish and stock from the bowl into a warm serving bowl. Garnish with the prepared spring onion on the top.

Serve immediately.

PREPARATION TIME:	COOKING TIME	SERVES	SPICE RATING
15 MINS	10-12 MINS	2 PEOPLE	

ปลา 3 รส
PLA 3 ROS

PAN FRIED SEA BREAM WITH THREE FLAVOURED SAUCE

INGREDIENTS

2 sea bream fillets, pin boned

2 tbsp vegetable oil

FOR THE SAUCE

10g long red chillies, cut into 2.5cm long pieces

10g red pepper, chopped

10g garlic

15g shallots or red onion

10g coriander root or stork cut into short length

1½ tsp fish sauce

50g sugar

3 tbsp Nam Makarm Piek, tamarind juice (see page 186)

½ tbsp oil

TO GARNISH

2 long red chillies, thinly stripped

1 large sprig coriander

The sauce is what makes this dish so tasty, with a balance of spicy, sour and sweet flavours all at once.

METHOD

Chop all of the herbs and spices roughly on a large chopping board, or blend coarsely together in a food processor. Transfer to a bowl.

In a non stick wok, put the oil on a medium heat. Stir in the blended herbs until the aroma is released.

Then add the fish sauce, sugar and 2-3 spoonfuls of tamarind to begin with.

Once sugar has dissolved, taste, and add more seasoning if required.

This sauce should be a balance of spicy, sour and sweet flavours. Keep the sauce warm.

Heat a tablespoon of the vegetable oil in a frying pan over a medium to high heat. Season the fish on both sides with a pinch of salt then place into the pan with the skin facing down.

Fry the fish for 4-5 minutes or until the skin is crisp and golden brown, and the flesh is beginning to turn opaque around the edges.

Turn the fish over and cook for a further 1-2 minutes, or until the fish is completely cooked through.

Serve the sauce on a warm serving plate.

Lay the pan fried sea beam on the top and garnish with the coriander and red chillies.

PREPARATION TIME:	COOKING TIME	SERVES	SPICE RATING
15 MINS	20 MINS	2 PEOPLE	

ปลาหมึกผัดกะเพรา
PLA MEUK PAD KRAPOW
STIR-FRY SQUID WITH HOLY BASIL LEAVES AND THAI CHILLI

This fiery stir-fry will have you reaching for the water jug! Often served over steamed fragrant rice accompanied by a crispy fried egg as a one plate meal.

INGREDIENTS

200g prepared squid

2 tbsp vegetable oil

1 clove garlic, coarsely chopped

1-2 fresh Thai chillies, coarsely crushed

½ long red chilli, sliced diagonally

1 tbsp oyster sauce

¼ sugar

2-3 tbsp water, for sauce

½ handful white onion, thinly sliced

Small handful Thai holy basil leaves

METHOD

In a saucepan, bring two cups of water to boil. Blanch the squid for a few seconds. Drain and leave them aside.

Heat a wok on a medium heat, put the oil in and fry the garlic until golden brown. It should give a nice aroma, but be careful not to burn.

Add both of the chillies and squid, then turn the heat up to very high, stirring continuously for about 1 minute.

Add the oyster sauce and sugar. Drop a few spoonfuls of water in to make a gravy.

Stir in the white onion and long red chilli. Cook for a further 30 seconds.

Remove from the heat and add the holy basil leaves. Gently fold them into the stir-fry and serve immediately

CHEF'S TIP

Peel the thin layer of film from the inside of the squid. It will not shrink and will remain soft.

PREPARATION TIME:	COOKING TIME	SERVES	SPICE RATING
10 MINS	4-5 MINS	2 PEOPLE	

หอยเชลล์ผัดน้ำพริกเผา

HOY SHELL PAD NAM PRIK POW

FRESH SCALLOPS STIR-FRIED IN CHILLI OIL

INGREDIENTS

6 fresh scallops, off the shell

2 tbsp vegetable oil

1 small clove garlic, coarsely chopped

4 tsp Nam Prik Pow, chilli oil (see page 186)

1 fresh Thai chilli, coarsely crushed

2 tbsp oyster sauce

2 tsp light soy sauce

1 tsp sugar

3 tbsp water

75g white onion, thinly sliced

1 small handful sweet basil leaves

1 long red chilli, cut into fine strips lengthways

CHEF'S TIPS

Do not poach the scallops too long as they will be cooked again with the sauce. The end texture should be springy when touched. This is a hot dish, leave out the crushed chilli if less heat is preferred.

When travelling to the seaside for the day the topic of discussion will quickly turn to which restaurant to eat in and what dishes will be ordered. This is always high on the list!

METHOD

Bring two cups of water to the boil on high heat.

Poach the scallops for about 1-2 minutes.

Remove them from the wok and discard the water.

Dry the wok and put it back on a high heat.

Put the oil in and fry the garlic to release the aroma.

Add the oyster sauce, chilli oil, crushed chilli, light soy sauce and sugar.

Add water to make a more runny sauce and mix well.

Taste. It should be spicy at first, followed by saltiness. Season if necessary.

Stir-fry for about 1-2 minutes then add the poached scallops and white onion. Stir-fry for a further minute and turn off the heat. Mix in the long red chilli strips and then gently fold in the sweet basil.

Serve.

PREPARATION TIME:	COOKING TIME	SERVES	SPICE RATING
10 MINS	4-5 MINS	2 PEOPLE	🌶🌶🌶

RICE AND NOODLES

Steve and I love exploring the bustling street food scene all over Thailand but especially in Bangkok. Most urbanized Thais eat out on a daily basis, especially during lunchtime when reasonably priced and excellent quality one plate meals are readily available. The best street food vendors and cafés specialise in just one or two dishes and will have probably been trading for generations.

ผัดไทยกุ้ง
PAD THAI GUNG
PRAWN THAI STYLE SPECIAL FRIED NOODLES WITH TAMARIND SYRUP

This is often thought of as Thailand's national dish, and a lot of varieties of pad Thai are now hugely popular across the globe, although it is hard to beat the street food stalls lining the streets in Thailand!

INGREDIENTS

1 handful or 150g 3mm noodles, soaked
4-5 king prawns, shelled and de-veined
2 tbsp vegetable oil
2 medium sized eggs
1 tbsp light soy sauce
1 tbsp red onion, thinly sliced
½ tbsp pickled turnip
7-8 small cubes tofu, fried
2 tbsp Nam Makharm, tamarind syrup sauce (see page 186)
80g bean sprouts
15g chinese chives or spring onions, cut into 2cm length
1 lime wedge
½ tbsp ground peanut
1 pinch roasted dry chilli flakes (optional)

ALTERNATIVE FOR TAMARIND SYRUP

1 tbsp white (spirit) vinegar
1 tbsp sugar
1 drop dark soy sauce

CHEF'S TIP

Leftover uncooked soaked noodles can be kept in the freezer. The tamarind sauce can also be made in advance and kept in the fridge for a while in an airtight container.

METHOD

Soak noodles in tap water overnight.

Drain the water off and rinse in a colander.

Heat the oil in a wok on a medium to high heat.

Add the prawns and red onion. Stir for about 1 minute and then break in the eggs.

Turn the heat to very high, stirring all the time until the eggs are cooked.

This should take about 1 minute.

Add the soaked noodles, light soy sauce then put the pickled turnip and fried tofu in.

Continue cooking until the noodles are soft then spoon the tamarind sauce in, and mix thoroughly for 2 minutes.

(Alternatively, add the white vinegar, sugar and dark soy and mix thoroughly for 2 minutes)

Add the bean sprouts and Chinese chives (or spring onions) and mix well for 30 seconds.

Serve on a warm serving plate, with a wedge of lime, ground peanut and dry chilli flakes, if you like it spicy.

PREPARATION TIME: 20 MINS PLUS SOAK OVERNIGHT	COOKING TIME 5 MINS	SERVES 1 PEOPLE	SPICE RATING

ก๋วยเตี๋ยวผัดขี้เมาเนื้อ

GOYTEAW PAD KIMOW NUA

'DRUNKEN' NOODLE STIR-FRY BEEF AND TAMARIND SYRUP

INGREDIENTS

150g or 1 handful 10mm rice noodles

80g rump steak, thinly sliced

2 medium eggs

2 tbsp vegetable oil

1 tsp or 1 large clove garlic, coarsely chopped

1 red Thai chilli, coarsely chopped

1 tbsp oyster sauce

½ tbsp light soy sauce

1 tsp dark soy sauce

1 tsp sugar

2-3 tbsp water

100g Thai broccoli, cut into 5cm lengths

TO GARNISH

Crispy Krapow, holy basil leaves (see page 29)

CHEF'S TIP

Ensure that the heat is on full to achieve a slightly smoky flavour, but be careful not to burn.

Despite the name there is no alcohol in the ingredients of this dish - but when people are drinking with friends in Thailand a spicier and stronger tasting dish is preferred. These dishes are known as 'drunken' and have now become a style of dish in their own right. They are perfect if you are looking for something with a real kick to it.

METHOD

Soak the noodles in tap water overnight, making sure they are completely submerged.

Drain the water off and rinse. Put the soaked noodles in a colander to drain.

Heat the oil in a wok on medium heat. Stir the garlic in until the aroma is released and add the eggs, stirring continuously.

Turn the heat up to very high. Add the chilli and beef and stir to mix well with the rest of the ingredients in the wok. This should take about 2 minutes for the beef to be just done.

Add the noodles and stir really well to get noodles wrapped with heat. Be careful not to break or chop the noodles.

Every now and then, stir and leave the noodles to soften for about 4-5 minutes. Add half of the water at first.

Once the noodles are soft, add the seasoning and mix well. Taste and check the texture of noodles again. Add more water if required, and then stir.

Add the Thai broccoli at the end, once you are satisfied with the flavour and texture.

Cook the broccoli for 1 minute to get an al dente texture to the vegetable.

Serve on a warm serving plate and garnish with crispy basil leaves.

PREPARATION TIME:	COOKING TIME	SERVES	SPICE RATING
10 MINS PLUS OVERNIGHT FOR SOAKING	7-8 MINS	1 PERSON	

ข้าวผัดไก่
KOW PAD GAI
FRIED RICE WITH CHICKEN

A tasty and filling one plate meal.

INGREDIENTS

1 cup cooked steamed fragrant rice (see page 166)

75g chicken breast, thinly sliced

2-3 tbsp cooking oil

2 medium sized eggs

1 small clove garlic, coarsely chopped

1 tbsp oyster sauce

Pinch sugar

25g white onion, thinly sliced

15 spring onions, thinly sliced

2-3 cherry tomatoes, cut in half

TO SERVE

1 tbsp Prik Nam Pla, fish sauce with chilli (see page 187)

Few slices cucumber

1 fresh spring onion, thinly sliced

CHEF'S TIP

Spoon the fiery Prik Nam Pla over the fried rice to the desired level of spiciness. Top with a crispy fried egg if you are feeling hungry!

METHOD

Heat the oil in a wok on a medium heat. Fry the garlic and stir until the aroma is released and it is light golden brown.

This will only take about 30 seconds.

Add the egg and mix in, then turn the heat to full and add the chicken.

Stir-fry for about 3 minutes until the chicken is cooked then add the rice and all of the seasoning. Mix thoroughly.

Put all of the onions and tomatoes in, mix well for 1 more minute, then remove from the heat.

Using a small bowl as a mould, push in the finished rice and turn it over onto a warmed serving plate. Serve with a few slices of cucumber, a fresh spring onion and a small bowl of Prik Nam Pla, the fish sauce with chilli.

PREPARATION TIME:	COOKING TIME	SERVES	SPICE RATING
15 MINS	7 MINS	1 PERSON	

ข้าวซอย

KOW SOI

NORTHERN CURRY NOODLES WITH CHICKEN

The blend of warm chicken curry noodles with the fresh garnish ingredients creates a lovely contrast in texture, and adds a few extra layers of fresh flavour.

INGREDIENTS

50g chicken breast, thinly sliced (alternatively use 1 drumstick)

1½ tbsp yellow curry paste

60g dry yellow noodles

½ tbsp vegetable oil

200ml coconut milk

1 tsp sugar

1 tsp fish sauce

¼ cup water

TO GARNISH

1 tbsp red onion, thinly sliced

10g pickled cabbage, very thinly sliced

1 tsp Nam Prik Pow, chilli oil (see page 186)

1 wedge lime

½ handful crispy fried egg noodles (optional)

1 sprig coriander

METHOD

Soak the dried noodles in warm water until soft and easy to separate. Once softened, drain in a colander.

In a saucepan on high heat, put the oil and curry paste in. Stir for 30 seconds and add 3-4 tablespoons of the thick part of the coconut milk. Mix well until the aroma is released.

Quickly add the rest of the coconut milk and bring it to boil. This takes about 2 minutes.

Put the chicken in and the cook for about 3-4 minutes.

Add water and season with the fish sauce and sugar. Mix well and taste.

Add more water and seasoning if required. Once satisfied with the curry sauce consistency, keep warm.

In another saucepan on a high heat, bring the water to boil.

Cook the soaked noodles until done. This does not take long and can be just poach boiled for an al dente texture.

Be aware that some noodle brands are labeled as 'easy to cook', and will require less time. Have a colander ready to drain the poached noodles really well.

Serve in a warm bowl and pour the chicken curry sauce on the top.

Sprinkle the red onion, cabbage, crispy egg noodles and coriander on top.

Drizzle with chilli oil to the desired spice level and squeeze the lime wedge over just before eating.

PREPARATION TIME:	COOKING TIME	SERVES	SPICE RATING
10-15 MINS PLUS 30 MINUTES FOR THE CURRY PASTE	13-15 MINS	2 PEOPLE	

ข้าวคลุกกะปิ
KOW KLUK KAPI
FRIED RICE WITH SHRIMP PASTE

INGREDIENTS

3 cups cooked rice (see page 166)
1 small clove garlic
2 tsp shrimp paste
1 tbsp dried prawns
1 tbsp coconut milk
1 tbsp vegetable oil

FOR THE SWEET PORK BELLY

80g pork belly, sliced into 1½cm pieces
½ tsp cinnamon powder
½ cup water
1½ tbsp oyster sauce
½ tsp dark soy sauce
2 tbsp palm sugar or brown sugar

FOR THE ACCOMPANIMENTS

25g or 2 tbsp shredded sour green mango
2 shallots, thinly sliced
25g fried sweet pork sausage, cut diagonally into ½ cm pieces (optional)
½-1 fresh Thai chilli, finely cut
2 wedges lime
½ tbsp veg oil
1 egg to make thinly shredded omelette
1 tsp chilli oil
1 wedge lime
½ handful crispy fried egg noodles (optional)
1 sprig coriander

This fried rice is quite unusual as shrimp paste is the main seasoning in this dish. It might not sound appetising but it is truly scrumptious. The fried rice is accompanied by sweet belly pork, shredded omelette, shallots and shredded sour green mango, which add an extra layer of flavour and crunchy textures into the dish.

METHOD

Start this recipe by making the sweet belly pork. Put all the ingredients, except for the sugar, together in a saucepan and bring to the boil.

Reduce the heat to simmering and leave to tenderise for about 25 minutes. The water should by now reduce to cover the pork belly.

Then add the sugar and continue simmering until it is all dissolved. Stir well to season and cover all of the pork pieces for about 5 minutes. The pork should be nice and shiny with a slight syrupy sauce consistency.

While the the pork belly is simmering, if you have not yet cooked the fragrant rice, do so now.

Prepare the rest of the ingredients and assemble the fried rice ingredients ready to stir-fry.

Once the rice is cooked, scoop the right amount into a bowl and leave aside.

In a wok, heat the oil on a medium heat and make the omelette, then slice it thinly. Put this aside in a small bowl.

If you are having the sweet pork sausage, stir them in the wok on a medium heat without any oil for 1-2 minutes. Leave aside.

In the same wok, add one tablespoon of vegetable oil and fry the garlic until the aroma is released, and they turn a light golden brown.

Add the shrimp paste and coconut milk, then stir vigorously to separate the paste and mix well.

Add the dried prawns and cooked rice.

Turn the heat up to high and stir to mix well. This will only take a few minutes.

Divide the fried rice into two bowls and press firmly before turning them upside down onto two warm serving plates.

Arrange all of the accompaniments around the fried rice and serve.

PREPARATION TIME:	COOKING TIME	SERVES	SPICE RATING
15 MINS	30 MINS	2 PEOPLE	

RICE

Thailand is a rice growing country where almost everybody eats rice at least once a day. Hence housewives up and down the country are experts at selecting, cooking and serving a good bowl of rice to accompany the family meals.

When I was young my mother would cook the rice over a charcoal burner but getting the perfect steamed rice this way is becoming very rare in Thailand. Electric rice cookers are universally used and every household has one as we would an electric kettle.

With an electric rice cooker you can get the perfect rice every time and it will also be kept warm until your other dishes are ready, meaning one less thing to think about when preparing a meal!

In order to achieve fluffy rice with each grain separate, always rinse the rice 3 times in cold water and accurately fill the water to the correct level. There will be markings on the side of the rice cooker bowl corresponding to the number of cups of rice being cooked. Press the button and that's it - you will have fluffy warm rice whenever you need it!

KOW NEOW

STICKY RICE

Sticky or glutinous rice is a different variety of rice than steamed, fragrant rice. It is very sticky when cooked, and can form a single clump. Traditionally it is eaten with your fingers by pulling off smaller clumps to accompany barbecued meat, fish, salads and spicy dips.

INGREDIENTS

1 cup Thai glutinous rice

1 cup of water

CHEF'S TIP

Try to be as accurate as possible with the water. Too much will make the rice too wet and mushy.

If it is too dry, sprinkle a few drops of water in and continue cooking for a few minutes longer.

METHOD

Soak the glutinous rice with lukewarm water for 3 hours, or with tap water overnight.

Ensure that the rice is completely submerged and has enough water to remain covered when it expands during soaking.

When ready, pour the soaked rice in a fine sieve and rinse it under fresh cold tap water.

Shake as much water out as possible. This is to be more accurate with the water measured for cooking it.

Put the rinsed glutinous rice in a Pyrex dish and cover with 1 cup of water. Place the lid on.

In a microwave on full power, cook for 5 minutes.

Take out and stir gently, using a wooden spoon to work around the bowl and underneath the rice to fold it in.

Return to the microwave immediately and cook for a further 2 minutes.

Remove and check the colour of the rice grains.

When they are all translucent, the rice will be cooked. If some are still white, cook for a further minute, or until they are done.

Be careful of the hot steam that will escape when opening the lid.

PREPARATION TIME:	COOKING TIME	SERVES
3 HOURS OR SOAK OVERNIGHT	8-12 MINS	2 PEOPLE

DESSERTS

Thai desserts may be unusual for a western palate, combining savoury aspects such as rice and chilli with sweet or sour fruits. Quite often they are not eaten after a meal, and are enjoyed as a snack. Here are a selection of desserts which are likely to appeal to western tastes.

PEANUT BUTTER CREME BRÛLÉE WITH BANANA AND PEANUT BRITTLE

A familiar dessert with a Thai twist.

INGREDIENTS

600ml double cream

¾ cup caster sugar

½ tsp ground cinnamon

4 large egg yolks

5 tsp cornflour

1 tsp vanilla extract

½ cup smooth peanut butter

FOR THE TOPPING

1 large ripe banana

6 small pieces of peanut brittle

6 tbsp brown Demerara sugar

METHOD

On a low heat, put the double cream, sugar, ground cinnamon and the peanut butter in a saucepan. Heat the cream mixture gently and occasionally stir with a wooden spoon for 6-7 minutes or until a little bubbling appears around the edge of the saucepan.
Remove it from heat immediately.
While heating the cream, use a balloon whisk to whisk together the egg yolks, vanilla extract and cornflour in a mixing bowl, with a cloth underneath to steady it.
When the cream mixture is ready, temper the egg yolks by whisking the egg mixture all the time with one hand and gradually pouring the hot cream a little by little at first and then all into the bowl.

Make sure you are whisking continuously.
Then, immediately pour the mixture back to the saucepan and put it back on a low gentle heat.
Continue whisking until the custard is thick and smooth. This will take about 4-5 minutes.
If the mixture is too thick, whisk quite vigorously until it becomes smooth again.
Immediately pour the custard mixture into 6 ramekins. Gently tap the ramekins on a piece of thick cloth to allow the contents to settle with a smooth surface.
Leave to cool on a big rack and cover each dish with cling film to refrigerate overnight.
Before serving, slice the banana very thinly. Arrange them neatly on the top of the chilled custard. Sprinkle a teaspoon of Demerera sugar. Use a cook's blowtorch to heat the sugar by moving it quickly and evenly over the surface, wait for 20 seconds and repeat if necessary.
Serve each bowl with a piece of peanut brittle.

PREPARATION TIME:	COOKING TIME	SERVES
15 MINS +	10-12 MINS	6 PEOPLE
REFRIGERATE OVERNIGHT		

ข้าวเหนียวมะม่วง
KOW NEOW MAMMUANG
MANGO WITH SWEET STICKY RICE

Mangos are very popular in Thailand, so much so Bangkok is affectionately known as 'The Big Mango'. This dessert can be regarded as the national dessert of Thailand – combining fresh sweet fragrant mango and sweetened coconut sticky rice.

INGREDIENTS

½ cup Thai glutinous rice

½ cup of water

3 tbsp thick part of coconut milk

3 tbsp granulated sugar

1 pinch of salt

1 tsp roasted sesame seeds

2 large sweet mangos

METHOD

Soak the glutinous rice in lukewarm water for 3 hours or tap water overnight.

Ensure that the rice is submerged and that there is enough water for it to remain covered when rice expands during soaking.

When ready, pour the soaked rice in a fine sieve and rinse it under fresh cold tap water.

Shake as much water out as possible.

Put the rinsed glutinous rice in a Pyrex dish and cover with half a cup of water. Place the lid on.

In a microwave on full power, cook for 4 minutes at first.

Try a grain of rice; it should be cooked (translucent) but still firm. Cook for a further 1 minute if necessary.

In a small saucepan over a low heat, gently heat the coconut milk, sugar and salt until dissolved. Do not overheat as the oil will separate out of the coconut milk.

Pour over the hot sticky rice, mix and leave to soak in completely.

Peel the mango and then slide a knife blade along each side of the large stones inside to separate it from the fruit. Slice the fruit into 1½ cm pieces and arrange on three serving plates. Divide the sticky rice into three and serve with the mango. Sprinkle with sesame seeds.

PREPARATION TIME:	COOKING TIME	SERVES
3 HOURS OR SOAK OVERNIGHT	8-12 MINS	3 PEOPLE

ไอศครีมมะม่วง
MANGO SUNDAE

This is a modern variation of the Kow Neow Mammuang, mango with sticky rice.

INGREDIENTS

½ cup Thai glutinous rice

½ cup of water

3 tbsp thick part of coconut milk

3 tbsp granulated sugar

1 pinch of salt

1 tsp roasted sesame seeds

2 ripe sweet mangos

8 scoops coconut ice cream

4 mint leaves for garnish (optional)

METHOD

TO MAKE THE SWEET STICKY RICE

Soak the glutinous rice in lukewarm water for 3 hours or tap water overnight.

Ensure that the rice is submerged and has enough water to remain covered when it expands during soaking.

When ready, pour the soaked rice in a fine sieve and rinse it under fresh cold tap water.

Shake as much water out as possible.

Put the rinsed glutinous rice in a Pyrex dish and cover with half a cup of water. Place the lid on.

In a microwave on full power, cook for 4 minutes at first.

Try a grain of rice, it should be cooked (translucent) but still firm. Cook for a further 1 minute if necessary.

In a small saucepan over a low heat, gently heat the coconut milk, sugar and salt until dissolved. Do not overheat as the oil will separate out of the coconut milk.

Pour over the hot sticky rice, mix and leave to soak in completely.

TO MAKE THE SUNDAE

Peel the mango and then slide a knife blade along each side of the large stone inside to separate it from the fruit. Dice the fruit into 1cm cubes.

Purée a third of the mango and leave this aside.

Using four sundae glasses, spoon one tablespoon of warm sweet sticky rice into the bottom of each glass.

Divide half of the remaining diced mango on the top of the sticky rice, followed by two scoops of coconut ice cream.

Place the rest of the mango in and pour the mango purée on the top. Garnish each with a mint leaf and serve.

PREPARATION TIME:	COOKING TIME	SERVES
3 HOURS OR SOAK OVERNIGHT	15 MINS	4 PEOPLE

กล้วยบวชชี
GLUAY BUADCHEE
BANANA IN COCONUT MILK

INGREDIENTS
1 ripe banana, medium sized

200ml coconut milk

1 tbsp sugar

1 pinch salt

My mum never fails to serve us this on the first few days of our arrival to Thailand! She uses smaller 'Nam Wah' bananas which are firmer and have a lovely aftertaste. There are over 30 varieties of bananas in Thailand and they are thought to originate in the south of the country. Thais believe that bananas signify abundant food, a long and prosperous life and a big, united family and hence are often used as offerings at homes, businesses and weddings.

METHOD
Shake the coconut tin to get the right consistency of both the thick and liquid parts of the coconut milk

Put the required amount in a saucepan along with the sugar and salt.

Bring to the boil on a medium heat for about 3 minutes. Taste and add more seasoning if required.

This should be a sweet taste with just a hint of saltiness.

Slice the banana diagonally about 1cm thick and put them in the boiling coconut. Cook for a further 2 minutes.

Pour into a small bowl and serve immediately.

PREPARATION TIME:	COOKING TIME	SERVES
5 MINS	5 MINS	1 PERSON

SAUCES & PASTES

The paste recipes that follow provide the base to the curries in the book. The sauces vary from ingredients within a main meal to the classic sweet chilli dipping sauce, which is delicious as an accompaniment. It is always a good idea to have these made up in advance before you begin preparing your meal to save time. You can even keep them in the fridge in an airtight container for a few days.

KREUANG GAENG DAENG
Red curry paste

Preparation time: 20 mins
Makes 4 tbsp
Spice rating 3

Ingredients

5 large dried whole chillies, cut into 2-3cm pieces and soaked
1 tsp salt
5g galangal, finely sliced
1 tbsp lemongrass, finely sliced
1 tbsp kaffir lime zest
1 tbsp coriander seeds
1 tbsp white peppercorn
1 tsp ground fennel
1 tbsp coriander roots, finely cut
4 shallots, finely sliced
6 cloves garlic, thinly sliced
1 tsp shrimp paste

Method

In a dry frying pan on a medium heat, put in the coriander seeds to roast. Stir or move the pan around continuously for 1 minute so the seeds won't burn. The seeds will crackle and pop a little. The colour will change to darker brown and a light fragrant aroma will be released.

Turn off the heat and remove the seeds out of the pan immediately into a small bowl. Leave it to cool.

In a heavy granite mortar and pestle, pound the white peppercorn until very fine. Add the cooled roasted coriander seeds. Pound them together into a really fine powder and spoon it into a small bowl.

Drain and squeeze out any water from the chilli and add to the mortar along with the salt. Pound them until fine.Add the galangal, lemongrass, kaffir lime zest and coriander roots, and pound each addition one by one until it makes a really fine paste.

Add the powdered ingredients to the wet paste and pound further.

Add the shallots, garlic and shrimp paste and pound one by one into a fine paste.

KREUANG GAENG KEO WAN
Thai green curry paste

Prep time 1 hour
Makes 180g or 8 tbsp
Spice rating 3

Ingredients

10 fresh long green chilies
5 Thai small green chillies
1 tsp salt
10g fresh galangal finely sliced
1 tbsp sliced fresh lemongrass,
1 tsp finely kaffir lime zest
1 tsp chopped coriander root
5 white peppercorns
1 tbsp dry roasted coriander seeds
1 tsp dry roasted cumin seeds
5 shallots, sliced
5 big cloves garlic
1 tsp shrimp paste

Method

In a dry frying pan on medium heat, put in the coriander seeds to roast for 1 minute. Stir or move the pan around continuously so the seeds don't burn. The seeds will crackle and pop a little.

The colour will change to darker brown and a light fragrant aroma will be released.

Turn off the heat and remove the seeds out of the pan immediately into a small bowl. Leave to cool.

Put the pan back on the heat and repeat the same process with the cumin seeds.

Pound together in a mortar and pestle until you get a fine powder. Add the peppercorns and pound very finely.

Transfer to a small bowl.
Cut both types of green chilli into a very fine slices.
Put the prepared chilli and salt in the mortar and pound until very fine.
Add the galangal, lemongrass, kaffir lime zest and coriander root, one by one pounding each addition until it makes a really fine paste.
Now add the bowl of powdered ingredients and pound again.
Add the shallots, garlic and shrimp paste one by one, again pounding into a fine paste after each addition.

KEUANG GAENG PANEANG
Panaeng curry paste
Preparation time 30 mins
Makes 4 tbsp
Spice rating 3
Ingredients
4 large dried chillies, cut into 2-3cm lengths and soaked in water
2 small dried chillies, soaked
1 tsp salt
1 tbsp galangal finely sliced
1 tsp ground nutmeg
½ tsp white peppercorns
1 tbsp coriander root, finely sliced
1 tbsp lemongrass, thinly sliced
1 tsp kaffir lime zest
5 shallots, peeled
3 small cloves garlic
½ tsp white pepper
½ tsp shrimp paste
Method
In a heavy granite mortar and pestle, pound the white peppercorn until very fine and transfer to a small bowl. Leave aside.
Put the prepared chilli, drain and squeezed out any water in the mortar along with the salt. Pound them until very fine.
Add the galangal, lemongrass, kaffir lime zest and coriander root, one by one pounding each addition until a really fine paste. Now add the ground nutmeg and white pepper, pounding to mix in well.

Add the shallots, garlic and shrimp paste one by one, again pounding into a fine paste after each addition.

KREUANG GAENG MASSAMAN
Massaman curry paste
Preparation time 30 mins
Makes 2 tbsp
Ingredients
4 big dried Thai chillies, de-seeded, soaked and drained
1 tsp salt
2 tsp or 4-5 slices galangal, thinly sliced
2 tbsp or 1 stalk lemongrass
4 shallots, thinly sliced
2 cloves garlic, thinly sliced
½ tsp whole white peppercorns, finely ground
1 tsp roasted cumin seeds, finely ground
1 tsp roasted coriander seeds, finely ground
3 cardamom seeds, finely ground
5 cloves, ground
1 dried bay leaf, torn into small pieces and finely ground
½ tsp shrimp paste
Method
Soak the cut chilli with boiling water in a small bowl for 4 -5 minutes. Squeeze out the water when ready.
Meanwhile, in a frying pan on a medium heat, put in the coriander seeds to dry roast. Stir or move the pan around continuously so the seeds won't burn. This will only take a minute or two. The seeds will crackle and pop a little. The colour will change to a darker brown and a light fragrant aroma will be released.
Turn off the heat and immediately place the seeds in a small bowl. Leave to cool.
Put the pan back on the heat and repeat the same process with the cumin seeds.
Pound them together until they make a really fine powder in a heavy granite mortar and pestle. Spoon it into a bowl.
Grind all of the ingredients one by one and spoon into

the same bowl. Drain the chilli really well.
Put the drained chilli and salt in the mortar and pound until you make a very fine paste.

KREUANG GAENG KARI
Yellow curry paste
Preparation time 15-20 minutes
Makes 4 ½ tbsp
Ingredients
5 dried chillies, cut into 1cm long pieces
1 tsp salt
3-4 thin slices galangal
1 tbsp fresh lemongrass, finely sliced (use only the thick part of ½ stork)
3-4 thin slices ginger, peeled
7-8 shallots
5 garlic cloves, peeled
1 tbsp dry roasted coriander seeds
1 tsp dry roasted cumin seeds
2 tsp curry powder
2 tsp turmeric powder
1 tsp Thai shrimp paste (kapi)
Method
Soak the cut chilli in a small bowl of boiling water for 4 -5 minutes.
Meanwhile, in a frying pan on a medium heat, put in the coriander seeds to roast. Stir or move the pan around continuously so the seeds don't burn. This will only take a minute or two.
The seeds will crackle and pop a little and the colour will change to a darker brown, releasing a light fragrant aroma. Turn off the heat and remove the seeds and immediately place into a small bowl. Leave to cool.
Put the pan back on the heat and repeat the process with the cumin seeds. Pound them into a fine powder in a heavy granite mortar and pestle. Transfer to a small bowl.
Drain the chilli really well.
Put drained chilli and salt in the mortar and pound until it makes a very fine paste.
Start adding each ingredient one by one in the above sequence.
Makes about 4 ½ tablespoons of curry paste. If you're not

using them all, put portion into individual small freezer bags, which can be kept for a long time. Thaw naturally when needed.

KREUANG GAENG LEUANG
Southern yellow paste
Preparation time 10-15 minutes
Makes 2 tbsp
Ingredients
2 chillies cut into 1cm lengths, soaked and well drained
¼ salt
1 large clove garlic
2 shallots
¼ tsp or 3-4 thinly slices fresh turmeric
1 tsp shrimp paste
Method
In a heavy granite mortar, put drained chilli and salt in.
Pound it until very fine. This might take about 7-8 minutes.
Add the shallots, garlic and turmeric and pound into a really fine paste.
Add the shrimp paste last and then pound into the rest of the ingredients.

NAM JIM JAEW
Dipping sauce
Preparation time 10 mins
Serves 1-2
Spice rating 3
Ingredients
1 tbsp fish sauce
½ tsp sugar
½ tbsp freshly squeezed lime juice
½ tsp roasted dried chilli flakes
1 tsp ground roasted rice (see page X)
1 tsp spring onion, thinly sliced across
1 tsp coriander, finely cut
Method
In a small bowl, mix the fish sauce, sugar, lime juice and chilli flakes until all of the sugar is dissolved.
Spoon the spring onion and coriander in and mix together.
Sprinkle the ground roasted rice on just before serving to achieve a crunchy texture.

NAM PRIK POW
Chilli oil

Preparation time 15 mins
Cooking time 6 mins
Makes 200ml
Spice rating 3

Ingredients
4 tsp dried coarse chilli flakes
2 shallots, peeled
2 cloves garlic, peeled
2 tbsp dried shrimp
¼ tsp salt
12 tbsp vegetable oil

Method
Using a granite mortar and pestle, pound the dried shrimp until fine and powdery. Put it in a small bowl and leave it aside.
In the same mortar, pound the garlic until it becomes a fine paste. This will make about 2 teaspoons of garlic paste. Remove into a small bowl and leave it aside.
Repeat the same process with the shallots. And again this will make about 2 teaspoons of fine shallot paste.
In a frying pan, put the oil, dried shrimp powder, garlic and shallot paste in.
Start on a medium heat and then slowly reduce the heat down to low after a gentle aroma is released.
Stir continuously with a wooden spoon for 3 minutes. Put the salt in and continue cooking and stirring for a further 1-2 minutes on a low heat.
Make sure you only have a gentle bubbling boil. Do not overheat.
Stir in the coarsely dried chilli flakes and mix well for 1 more minute. Leave it to cool before putting in an airtight jar.
You should have about 200ml of chilli oil mixture.

NAM MAKHARM
Tamarind syrup sauce

Preparation time 20 -25 minutes
Cooking time 5 -6 minutes
Makes 1 litre of sauce
Spice rating 0

Ingredients
50g tamarind, in a block

250ml boiled water
1 tsp salt
375g sugar
½ tsp dark soy sauce

Method
Soak the tamarind with really hot water until it has softened. This will take about 15-20 minutes.
When the water is getting cooler or lukewarm, break the tamarind up with your hand, using a disposable glove.
Ensure the maximum amount has been dissolved in the water, which will be when you can see the tamarind stone appear.
Sieve the juice through a coarse sieve with a big bowl underneath.
Squeeze as much juice out as possible.
You will get about 200ml of tamarind juice.
To make the tamarind syrup sauce, pour the tamarind juice in a saucepan on a medium to high heat.
Add the sugar and salt. Stir continuously to ensure both ingredients dissolve.
Add the dark soy sauce and taste. This should be a balance of tangy, sweet and salty in the same strength. It should take about 5-6 minutes in total for a good syrupy consistency.
Leave it to cool and keep in an air tight jar in a fridge.

NAM JIM TALAY
Fresh chilli and garlic dipping sauce

Preparation time 15 minutes
Serves 3-4
Spice rating 3

Ingredients
50g mixed green and red Thai chillies
25g coriander roots or storks, thinly sliced
25g or 4 large cloves garlic
10g pickled garlic, drained and thinly sliced
2 tbsp sugar
3 tbsp fish sauce
3 tbsp fresh lime juice

Method
In a heavy mortar and pestle,

pound the chilli and fresh garlic together until broken up into small pieces.
Add the coriander and pickled garlic, then pound together.
Add all the seasoning and mix until the sugar is dissolved. If the mortar is small, transfer to a mixing bowl before adding the seasoning.
Taste a very small amount as this is a spicy sauce to eat on its own. It should initially taste spicy and tangy, followed by a balance of saltiness and sweetness.

NAM JIM ARJARD
Cucumber pickle

Preparation time 2 minutes
Cooking time 5 minutes
Makes 2 cups of sauce
Spice rating 1

Ingredients
1 cucumber
1 shallot
1 long red chilli
300g sugar
1 tsp salt
3 tbsp white vinegar
1 cup of water

Method
In a saucepan, bring the water to boil on a high heat.
Add the sugar and stir until dissolved. This should only take 30 seconds.
Add salt.
Leave it boiling until the consistency becomes like a very light syrup.
This may take about 4 minutes since it was placed over the heat
Add the vinegar and continue boiling for 1 more minute.
Taste. This is a light tangy syrup with the colour of white wine.

Method – pickle
Cut the cucumber in half and remove the centre part and seeds. Dice.
Slice the shallot or if using red onion, dice.
Finely slice the long red chilli.
Mix the prepared vegetables in a bowl and pour over the sauce to cover.

NAM MAKARM PIEK
Tamarind juice

Prep time 20-25 mins
Cooking time 0
Makes 200ml juice
Spice rating 0

Ingredients
50g tamarind in block
250ml boiling water

Method
Soak the tamarind with really hot water until it is soft. This will take about 15-20 minutes.
When the water is getting cooler or lukewarm, break the tamarind up with your hand, using a disposable glove.
Ensure the maximum amount is dissolved in the water; this will be when you can see the tamarind stone appear.
Sieve the juice through a coarse sieve with a large bowl underneath.
Squeeze as much juice as possible.

KRATIEM GROB
Crispy fried garlic

Preparation time 5-10 minutes
Cooking time 45-50 seconds

Ingredients
50-100g garlic, coarsely chopped
2-3 cups cooking oil

Method
Prepare a heatproof tray lined with a few pieces of kitchen paper.
Prepare another tray ready with kitchen paper to put the crispy fried garlic on to cool.
Heat the oil in a deep wok on a high heat.
When the oil is hot but not smoky, put the chopped garlic in.
Stir quickly to ensure the garlic will be evenly cooked and light golden brown and crispy.
This will only take less than 1 minute.
Turn the heat off and immediately remove the fried garlic from the hot oil.
Or alternatively, drain the garlic into a fine sieve with a heatproof bowl underneath.
Pour the sieved garlic onto the prepared tray to dry.

Make sure the garlic pieces are scattered evenly on the kitchen papers so that all of the oil drains off.

Leave it to cool before keeping it in an airtight container.

HOM JEOW
Crispy fried shallot
Preparation time 5-10 mins
Cooking time 45-50 seconds

Ingredients
50-100g shallots, peeled and thinly sliced.
2-3 cups cooking oil

Method
Line a heatproof tray with a few pieces of kitchen paper, ready for when the crispy fried shallots are done. They do not take long to cook.

Heat the oil in a deep wok on a high heat.

When the oil is hot but not smoky, put the sliced shallots in.

Stir quickly. Make sure the shallot pieces are completely submerged under the hot oil. This will help them to cook evenly, giving them a crisp texture and a very light golden brown colour. This will only take less than 1 minute.

Turn the heat off and immediately remove the fried shallots from the hot oil. Or alternatively, drain the fried shallots through a fine sieve with heatproof bowl underneath.

Pour the sieved shallots onto the prepared tray with kitchen paper to dry. Make sure the shallots are scattered on the kitchen paper evenly so that the maximum amount of oil is drained.

Leave to cool before keeping in an airtight container.

NAM JIM WAN
Sweet chilli sauce
Prep time 5 minutes
Cooking time 12- 13 minutes

Ingredients
10g long red chillies, cut and finely minced in a food processor
1 tsp salt
2 tbsp white vinegar
1 cup water

Method
In a saucepan, bring the water to boil on a high heat.

Add sugar and stir until it is dissolved. This should only take 30 seconds.

Add salt.

Leave it boiling until the consistency becomes syrupy. This may take about 7-8 minutes since it was first placed over the heat.

Pour in the vinegar and leave for a couple of minutes.

Then add the minced chilli and quickly turn the heat down. This is crucial as the sauce will rise quite high with lots of bubbles.

Simmer for a further 2 minutes after chilli goes in. This is a runnier and less spicy sauce than the plum one.

Leave it to cool completely and keep in an airtight jar. You will get just under a cup of mixture.

Chef's tips
Be very careful when you open the lid of food processor after mincing the chilli. Do not breathe in as this will make you choke or cough.

It might take a while to mince the chilli as big pieces will need more time.

If this is the case, use a spoon to scrape down and do another short whizz.

Remember to use disposable gloves to handling chilli.

NAM JIM BUAY
Sweet chilli sauce with preserved plum
Preparation time 5 mins
Cooking time 12-15 mins
Makes 1 cup of sauce
Spice rating 2

Ingredients
15g long red chilli, cut and quite finely minced
150g sugar
3 preserved plums, stone removed and broken up
1 tbsp plum juice
2 tbsp white vinegar
1 cup of water

Method
In a saucepan, bring the water to boil on high heat.

Add sugar and stir for 30 seconds, until it has dissolved.

Add the prepared plum and its juice.

Leave it boiling until you get a syrupy consistency. This may take about 8-10 minutes.

Pour in the vinegar and leave for 2-3 minutes then add the minced chilli and quickly turn the heat down. Heat control is crucial at this stage as the sauce will rise quite high with lots of bubbles.

Simmer for 2 minutes, after the chilli has gone in.

PRIK NAMPLA
Fish sauce with fresh chilli dip
Preparation time 3 mins
Serves 2
Spice rating 3

Ingredients
1-2 fresh red Thai chillies, cut into small pieces
1 small wedge fresh lime, cut into small pieces
1 tbsp fish sauce
A pinch sugar
A few thin slices garlic (optional)

Method
In a small sauce bowl, mix all of the ingredients together until the sugar is dissolved.

Chef's tip
For a vegetarian version use light soy sauce instead of fish sauce.

NAM JIM SATAY
Peanut sauce
Preparation time 1 min
Serves 2-4

Ingredients
½ tbsp red curry paste
150ml or ½ cup coconut milk
100g peanuts
1 ¼ tbsp sugar
¼ tsp salt
A pinch turmeric powder

Method
Stir all ingredients until some oil dots float on the top.

ACKNOWLEDGEMENTS

The road from my village in eastern Thailand to Chilli Banana restaurant in Wilmslow, Cheshire has been a truly enriching journey. This book has provided me with an opportunity to showcase many of my favourite recipes and to thank the people who have helped and supported me along the way.

I would like to pay tribute, first and foremost, to:

My beloved Mother who taught me the basics of Thai cookery and who encouraged me on this journey of discovery. She has nurtured and encouraged me from my early life growing up in Thailand, and from afar when I came to live in England, and has always been my inspiration and role model.

My father, who supported my education and travels and played an important role in my success.

My husband Steve, without whose support and passion for Thailand and Thai food, this book would have not been possible. His ability to interact with local people, coupled with an inquisitive mind has led to endless discoveries that I, as a native, would never have made!

My children Jasmine and Oliver have in their own way contributed to this book by enjoying my recipes and dishes from a very young age, and accompanying us on our many trips to this fascinating country.

My brothers and sisters and their families in Prachinburi for providing all the help I have ever needed when I am back home.

My in-laws, Tony and Elizabeth for their encouragement and enthusiasm.

My head chef Pi Saijai, and all of the Chilli Banana team for their fantastic hard work in the kitchen.

Tim Green for his beautiful photography, and now friendship.

To Nadia Raber and David Patrick for their input, help and support.

Mr and Mrs Boonpakdee for their invaluable knowledge of the herb gardens of Prachinburi.

Chu and Man Kullavanijaya for guiding us to and sharing with us so many amazing meals in the gourmet world of Bangkok.

My good friend Jayne Hindle for her willing and valued help.

For Helen and Tom, the best neighbours.

For Rachel, Phil, Paul and Marc at Meze Publishing for their patience and for making this book possible.

For the thousands of guests and friends who have visited Chilli Banana restaurants, for their feedback and comments and for leaving empty plates and returning again and again to try my new recipes!

And finally I thank, you the reader, for opening the pages of this book to share with me the magic of Thai cookery and the wonderful mouthwatering tastes of Thailand.